PATHWAYS

OF

PRAYER

MICHEL QUOIST

A new translation by
Hester Pemberton
with an introductory
commentary by
George Pattison

WILTON 65
2003

First Published in Great Britian
2003

by

WILTON 65
Hernes Keep, Winkfield, Windsor, Berkshire. SL4 4SY.

ISBN 0 947828 93 1

Pathways of Prayer

Chapter		Page

PREFACE

It is perhaps impossible to assess the influence exerted by a spiritual voice such as that of Michel Quoist. It is hard even to define that voice or to describe it to someone who has not heard it. For what is distinctive about Quoist is not the "message" his words contain, but their tonality or inflection. Quoist does not have a theological hypothesis to propound or a teaching to deliver. He does not speak to us as one who has new information to impart. Rather, he speaks with a reflective, observant, critical and self-critical candour that requires attention and thought but makes no noisy demands. If we are not drawn to pass this stretch of our journey in his company, if we have one or other objection to make to his view of things, then so be it, we are free to carry on along whatever way we want and he will not bluster or plead with us to come back. He does not seek students and still less disciples, but simply and humbly offers what he has seen, heard and thought as a gift to the Church, to his fellow human beings and – in, with and under that – to God.

When I was training for ordination in the 1970s it was hard to avoid Quoist. One or other of his books usually lay open on the prayer desk in the small college chapel and was the source or model for many students' first ventures in guiding the prayers of others. Perhaps at that time (or was it just that we were all young *men*?) it was the novelty – even the revolutionary quality – of these "prayers of life" that attracted and excited us. There was almost something iconoclastic about the way they blew away the mock-gothic cobwebs in which Christian, and especially Catholic, spirituality had become enveloped. There was a palpable toughness about the way Quoist staked out his ground right in the midst of the modern secular city that the most powerful theological voices were then pointing to as theology's new and future habitat. This was invigorating stuff, prayer for working people in a working, struggling world.

Yet Quoist's approach was not new for the sake of newness or revolutionary for the sake of striking dramatic poses. Least of all was he a "secular theologian" in the sense of demanding that the Church turn its back on a scriptural and traditional inheritance of concern for the inner life ("spirituality", if one will). The iconoclastic force of these prayers was itself but a reflection of the inexhaustibly positive refocusing of prayer on the concrete reality of contemporary life – with material as rich and as challenging as this, who needed dull manuals setting out the stages and phases and types of prayer!

I'll say it again: this was not "secular theology" in a negative sense. Quoist's absorption in the experiential and personal reality of life was not an abandonment of the Church's own agenda but a way of focussing and living out a deep, urgent love of God shaped by the example, teaching and person of the gospels' Christ. Jesus Christ is the central and constant partner-in-dialogue of these prayers. At one and the same time he remains recognizable as the Christ who walked and talked in Galilee and yet also one for whom the motorways, malls, high streets and back streets of the present-day city have become "roads to Emmaus" along which he passes, meeting those who are ready to recognize him for who he is and those who are not.

Don't be over-hasty in bracketing Quoist. He could sound like an arch conservative in unmasking the "I want" of the selfish modern West, but his respect for the integrity of each individual's freedom matches that of any modernist. He reads like an unreformed leftist in his affirmation of the values of co-operation, except for the accompanying insistence on individual self-scrutiny and effort. At times his championing of humanity might seem to eclipse God, until we remember that humanity serves Quoist as a window onto God. And if we are tempted to think that Quoist has become so taken up with the day-to-dayness of life that he has forgotten the darker and more difficult places of the spirit, look at the sharpness of the self-critique in "I am not afraid of you any more, Lord!" where the apparent brashness of the title is qualified by the admission that "I admit I was a bit afraid of you", and where the self-excusing question "Only a little bit, wasn't it?" is answered by the annihilating *But it was too much.*" And, if we think that all of this "spirituality" is the last thing needed in a world racked by real problems of hunger, war and disease, note the reflections on poverty in "He asked for 'a lemonade for two' " and the challenge it contains to a Church that is all too ready to moan if "their vicar" can't be present at every meeting or visit every parishioner but which sees no need for abundant human and economic resources to be directed to those in real material and spiritual wildernesses.

So, yes, "all human life is here", as a certain Sunday newspaper famously claims. There are no no-go areas in Quoist's way of prayer: shopping, washing, industry, travelling by train, the night shift, laddered stockings. Wherever we are, whatever we are doing - a moment's thought can make it hallowed ground. But there is the one condition: we must be thoughtful. Not because Quoist would turn us into intellectuals (far from it), but because thoughtfulness belongs to the inner essence of love. "Thinking of you" our messages to loved ones say, and Quoist's prayers are a training in the kind of thinking that love requires of us. The German philosopher Heidegger, for whom the meaning of thinking was a central philosophical issue, asked that the motto to his collected works be "ways (i.e. "paths") not works", hinting that thinking is a very different kind of thing from problem-solving. Real thinking does not reach "answers". It is as endless as life itself. Becoming thoughtful is a way of life, a way of being on life's way. So, too, Quoist's 'Chemins de Prières' – not a collection of prayers, or a manual of prayer or a guide to prayer, but "ways" of prayer. But (to say it once more) the "prayer" whose way this collection leads us down is no special aptitude that religious people alone have. It is as universal, as simple, and as difficult as thinking and loving.

We need, I said, to learn to listen not just to *what* Quoist says, but the tonality, the inflection, with which he says it. It is the miracle of good translation that words written in a language that is not our own can not only be rendered comprehensible, but that we seem to hear a real, authentic voice in the words printed on the page before us. This, I think, Hester Pemberton's translation does. And it does so because this was no mere translator's piece-work but something that grew out of her own spiritual life, a step in her own journeying along the way. No one is – perhaps no one should be – more invisible than a translator but, at least for those who knew her, the tone and tenor of Hester's own life has also shaped these words, a tone that – like Quoist's – bespeaks realism matched and transfigured by thoughtfulness and love.

George Pattison 2002

INTRODUCTION

Dear Friends,

We often tell ourselves:

I must pray because I "need to".
I want to pray but don't know how to.
I would like to pray, but I haven't got the time.
I want to pray more, but praying bores me and I lack the courage.

> *The hours pass and days and weeks pile up or stretch out and still this nagging desire, this profound dissatisfaction remains with us and goes on tormenting us from time to time. It can occur when a time of calm offers us a moment of peace after some violent upheaval, or on the other hand when, frustrated, wounded and thrown by the roadside, we cry 'Help!'.*

> *We search for God and would like to meet him to ask for his help. We need to pray, we do pray, but our prayer is difficult and we are not at all sure we have achieved anything?*

> *Do you know why our poor human efforts are often no more than a babble, which peters out; our prayers are to short to reach a God who seems to us too distant and invisible?*

> *Do you know why we become discouraged when our requests get no response, when God is deeply silent and there is night in our hearts?*

Do you know why our efforts to learn "how to pray" only succeed in making us eternal apprentices?

Do you know why all those routines repeated every day, the words and chants and the prostrations, the candles and incense ... and the thousand recommended practices will possibly one day be realized as nothing but sad illusions?
The fact is all these practices and efforts are as nothing if we don't first believe that it is God who has always "sought us" before we pray to him, that it is he who prays to us before we pray to him, that it is he who begs us to exhort him before we even begin to beseech him.

S John says to us "Herein is love, not that we loved God, but that he loved us, and sent his Son to be the propitiation for our sins".

John 1   4   v.10.

Everything is in this. God "so loved the world that he sent his Son" to be with us "every day till the end of time" (Matt 28 v.20). He stays, and accompanies us. He ceaselessly asks us to work with him and his Spirit of loving. And we, with our eyes shut too often, seek him in the sky, in the clouds of our fine ideas or in the flush of our fine feelings and our emotions. Then it is that we greatly risk missing him on his way.

Yes or no, do we believe that God came in Jesus Christ, a man like us, among us? Yes, we must receive him, and one of the best places to receive him must for us be the Gospel; certainly not the Gospel as a record of the actual words of Jesus of Nazareth, but as his essential message, collated by the apostles, meditated by the first Christian communities, authenticated by his Church. Through the Holy Scriptures, in a supreme way through the Gospels, God engages in dialogue with mankind. It is for mankind to respond; this is one of the essential foundations of Christian prayer.

But Jesus of Nazareth is dead. We believe that he is risen. He is alive today. His story is for us not ancient history, which one must only 'remember', it is a reality, mysterious for sure, but which unfolds through time. Jesus Christ continues to be born, to live, to suffer, to die, to rise again through his people. Our daily life in its smallest details, the lives of our brothers and sisters, individually and collectively the history of all humanity, are the second place of encounter and dialogue for mankind with God.

Alas too often we are blind and we don't see *Jesus Christ signalling to us through life. We are deaf and we don't* hear *him calling out to us in our daily routine. We must beg him to cure us of our blindness and deafness. then we will be able to talk to him, ceaselessly linking up the whole universe, all humanity with his action in the world, and little by little our lives will become a response of love which invites us.*

Certainly there are other paths of prayer, the liturgy, the sacraments, but if we detach our prayer from the Gospel and from life, we run a risk of setting off down blind alleys. They will lead us to illusion and disillusion. it is to enable some of us to avoid this danger that I offer you these pages.

For a long time very many readers of the first book Prayers of Life *have been asking for new ones. I have regularly refused, not wishing in any way to substitute my words for yours, my prayer for yours. Besides so many books have already appeared suggesting many texts to us. Should yet more be offered?*

If I have finally given in it is also because I am aware not of giving you anything but of restoring to you what the Lord and you yourselves have given me.

I have been seduced by Jesus Christ and I try to follow him. He speaks to me in the Gospel and I am fed by the word. But he also speaks to me through life, which I observe while going about, which you share with me. And 'I keep all these things in my heart' *and the words of my prayers are only attempts to respond to the Lord's repeated and urgent entreaty.*

I offer you some of these words pell-mell. They are mine, yours, and sometimes even Jesus', what I imagine Jesus would say to us if we could hear him with our worldly ears. In effect one must lend words to Jesus, who has no more to address us with in the changing complexity of our lives. If we are fed by the Gospel, we will gradually acquire the Gospel's reactions, and we can then with confidence ask ourselves the question 'what is Jesus Christ saying to me today, through this or this piece of my life or that of my brothers and sisters?' What does he expect of me, of us? Then one must reply by prayer and action.

I should have liked to offer you beautiful, very beautiful, words, worthy of the Lord and of you, but it would have taken much time, talent, and above all love, to formulate and fashion them even more fully, before offering them to you. I lack all that. But I console myself saying to myself that these prayers are only some paths to help you, if possible, to continue your pilgrimage to God, who came in Jesus Christ to the heart of our lives.

He is waiting for us!

Have a good journey my friends! Once again we could so easily miss him on the way seeking him where he is not. Or we can ceaselessly bind ourselves to him through life, our own, that of our brothers and sisters and of the world. Then all human history will become Prayer in Jesus Christ.

I
Glory to Thee my God!

Every man is happy when he is admired for himself, but he is often even more touched when the greatness of his work is sincerely appreciated. If he is a father his joy is at its peak when he is complimented on his children.

Why should God himself also not be pleased with this homage? Certainly it is right to glorify him for what he is, but not to forget to praise him for what he makes, and especially for his beloved children, men and women, with whom he is increasingly happy that they grow in the life that he has given them. Some people forget this, in the belief that they please him by not thinking of anything except him.

To glorify God through the man who grows is to be part of the loving proud gaze of our Father, he who does not take his eyes from his children, to the extent that 'not a hair of their head shall fall' without him noticing. 'The Glory', says St Irenaeus, 'is the living person – the life of a person – that is God'.

Glory to thee my God
for the little child who's learning to walk,
    drops his mother's hand
    falls
    gets up
    and again attempts the adventure,
for the boy on the bicycle
    who tries to ride without holding the handlebars
    and starts again twenty times without achieving it.
For the adolescent who struggles
    with his mathematical problem
    and works desperately
    because he wants to reach the solution on his own.

Glory to thee O God
for the sportsmen who train every day
    to run faster
    jump further
    and ever higher
    in order to beat their record.
For the artists who battle with stone or wood,
    colours or sounds,
    to create new works.
For the researchers who study and experiment in the dark
    to penetrate the secrets of this world
    which we inhabit together.

Glory to thee O God
for the miners who tear mineral from the earth,
    for those who melt it down
    and those who make tools
    and machinery,
for the architects and armies of masons
    who build houses, churches and towns,
for scholars, engineers, technicians,
    the multitude of workers
    spiritual and manual
    who slowly dominate the world and control life,
for all those who strive
    to develop mankind and nations
    and build a world of justice and peace.

Glory to thee, my God
for man who slowly raises himself up
    through the immensity of time;
since emerging from the clay
    you wanted him standing,
since the spark of soul was lit up in flesh,

you wanted him thinking, loving
and taking part in his own creation,
since liberated at last
you put the universe into his hands
 so that he could take possession of it
 fit it out and transform it.
 Glory to thee my God
for this prodigious and marvellous human climb
for your joy in seeing us grow
for your humility,
 you who efface yourself before us
 instead of taking us over,
for your patience at our slowness
 our mistakes, and our falls.

 Glory to thee my God
because you have created man free,
 and worthy of meeting you,
because you didn't think it demeaning
 to become yourself a man
 in your son Jesus
because through him
 if we desire it
 we can
 together say *Our Father*
 and one day come to you
 to live in your Love
 and your eternal Joy.

You are the light of the world…   *Matthew 5 vv 14-16*

Now unto him that is able to do exceeding abundantly …
           Ephesians 3 vv 20-21

II
LORD, WHY MUST ONE ALWAYS FORCE ONESELF?

Many young people and sometimes the not so young, rule their actions in accordance with their inclinations. For some it's a question more or less consciously, of refusal to make the effort, for others it is the firm conviction that in many circumstances they should not do what they don't want to do. To force oneself, they think, is not to be true to oneself, it's playacting, especially when it concerns other people, and even more when it concerns God: "if I don't want to I'm not going to smile at that person, pray, or go to mass."

This attitude is the fruit of a false conception of liberty and of bad education. It is thought to be respect for the liberty of the child, for his or her 'wishes:' he/she doesn't finish what he/she has on the plate 'because he/she doesn't want any more:' he/she won't say "good-bye"'to the lady 'because he/she doesn't want to:' he/she stops going to the catechism class 'because he/she doesn't want to go any more.'

The liberty that the Lord offers us is not the freedom to do anything we want but the freedom to love ourselves, other people and God Himself with this love, whatever our own wishes are.

Jesus Christ didn't 'want' to die for us.

Lord
why must one always force oneself?
> I don't want to.

I don't want to get up
> nor go to bed.

I don't want to go to work
> or to go to college.

I don't want to do the housework
> or to do the ironing.

4

I don't want to turn off the television
    and do my homework.
I don't want to hold my tongue
    nor to talk.
I don't want to go and see this person,
    to shake his/her hand
    nor even to smile at him/her.
I don't want to kiss him/her.
I don't want to do the favour asked,
    to get involved
    nor to go to this party.

I don't want to resist
    the lure of side tracks
    leading me off my way,
and don't want to extinguish those golden images
ceaselessly projected on the screen of my dreams.
I don't want to fight against time,
    to stop
    to reflect
    to meditate on your word
    and I don't want to pray to you.

Lord, why is it necessary always to force oneself
    to live each day
    as you wish us to live?
It isn't easy.
    It isn't fun.

So often I want to do
    what I should not do,
and so little want to do
    what I ought to do!

Lord,
is it true that one should always force oneself
    when one doesn't want to at all!

My child, says the Lord
    it is true,
that seed must be watered every day
    if there is to be a tree,
and it is true that a mother must travail for her child to be born,
    and parents must bring it up
    to grow into a man,
that the baker must work at night
    to knead the bread
and workers cooperate
for machinery to work
    even if they don't want to.

    It is true
that scholars must seek for a long time
to find the medicine that heals,
that men have to sacrifice their lives
    so that justice may come into being
and that lovers must every day die
to egoistical desires,
    so that love may endure
    even if they don't want to.

For where would be your dignity my child,
    your beautiful liberty
    and your ability to love
if the Father gave you the tree and the child ready made,
    and the healing medicine which never fails,
    and the universe like a paradise for a peaceful humanity,
    and let the lovers bloom like flowers

without any risk of fading.
It is difficult to be human,
    and difficult to love.
I know it.
I had no wish to climb
    towards the steps of Calvary for thirty years.
But my Father desired that my whole life,
    should be offered for you all,
And I, I loved you, my brothers and sisters,
    and if I forced myself
    to climb up on the cross
    it is so that all your efforts may one day,
    be crowned with *Life*.

Go, my child,
do not ask yourself if you want to do this or that,
ask yourself if the Father desires it
    for you and your brothers and sisters.
do not ask me for the strength to force yourself,
ask me instead to love with all your strength,
    both your God and your brothers and sisters.
For if you loved a little more
    you would suffer much less
and if you loved much more
    from your suffering joy would spring
    and at the same time *Life*.

The two brothers going or not going to work in the vineyard.

Matthew 21 vv 28-31

'He who would save his life will lose it.'   *Mark 8 vv 4-37*

III
THE BOIL WAS NOT READY, LORD, I SQUEEZED IT TOO SOON!

Educators want to 'form' those whom they educate. Devout and generous Christians want to 'do good' to those around them. Both one and the other they think they can 'from the outside' give them what they lack and free them from what they think is bad in them.
Our goodwill is often proud & intrusive.
Proud, because we see ourselves as wealthy and possessing all the answers, as opposed to others who are poor. Intrusive because the other person is primarily responsible for his own life and because no pressure from the outside can be justified. We need first to believe in the other person, in the life which dwells in him, to do everything to give value to it in his eyes. To help him to develop it rather than spending time wanting to rectify it, trying to detect the bad and root it out. Good grass which grows gradually smothers the brambles – say wise peasants.
And above all, we Christians must think and believe with all our strength that the Lord is there in the other person. It is he first of all whom we must allow to act. For he alone is the SAVIOUR who can destroy evil at its root and make life grow – his LIFE in our life.

The boil was not ready, Lord,
 I squeezed it too soon.
My patient suffered,
And his flesh was inflamed,
 but retained the poison.
I should have waited
 and gently cared for him,
waited for his body to be ready,
 and *he himself strong enough* to reject the infection.
So it is, Lord, that faced with him, and the others,
 who in their hearts suffer from an infected vein

8

I should have waited longer,
    and prayed at length.
    But I am
    as you know
    impatient,
    proud.
I should like to save my brothers
    before they agree to it
and themselves take arms
    against what is wrong with them.
And much more serious still –
    sure of my power,
    proud of my devotion,
I believe myself capable of healing the ill
    which you alone can heal.

Give me, above all, Lord,
    respect for the other person,
    and for his hidden life,
    in his long journey.
Never let me impose myself on a stranger –
    or even on my brother –
    if he himself
    does not open his door to me from the outside.

Give me the courage to wait,
    and not to hurl my words
    in concentrated bursts
    at the windows of a heart
    which is only half open.
For then these words will too often be shattered against the walls,
    and never reach the heart.

Unless some of them, more vivid and piercing
      penetrate the living flesh,
      wounding it even more cruelly.
Teach me Lord,
      silence
not empty silence
filled all too quickly with my foolish dreams,
but the silence which awaits a word from the other person,
      before gently slipping in my own.

Grant me humility,
      I who so often believe myself to be rich,
      in spite of my modest airs,
sure of my good-will
of my 'educator's' know-how
of my experience,
of my generosity,
even of my friendliness
and my all-powerful love.
I see myself as rich before the other person,
      who is for me a poor man,
whom I must enrich with my generous almsgiving.

Help me to know myself a sinner like him
      as I look at him,
      I who believe myself pure,
      I who am satisfied with my life
      which is decent in my eyes.
So proud I am of my small virtues,
      the meagre capital that I have been given,
      far more than I have ever earned.
Finally teach me Lord,
to pray as I look at the other person,

exposing him to the sun of your saving love,
    as I pray to you *in him*
    you who want to grow within him
    and in him desire
    to dwell forever.
For as for me, Lord,
    I have nothing to offer him,
    except your love, yours,
    through the feeble love which is mine,
    and my hand simply,
gently resting on his,
    and my peaceful gaze,
like a silent watcher
at the foot of the bed of a sick person,
    and perhaps a few words
    which will reach his heart,
if you in the night
    have put them on my lips ...

For I am nothing but your servant, Lord,
and if I am to take my duties,
    faithfully,
    humbly,
    conscientiously,
Attentive every day to the maladies of the souls
    which cross my path,
it is you only, who can assuage the ill
    in them
    in me
ill so profoundly buried
that no man's fingers squeezing it,
can make it emerge.

For you alone
can expel the infection
and heal the hearts.
Sometimes the bodies too are healed as well as hearts.

For *you alone are the Saviour*
and have come for that very purpose.

Judge not.   *Matthew 7 vv 1 & 3 vv 4–5*

The Kingdom of God is like seed.   *Mark 4 vv 26–29*

IV

OPEN MY EYES, LORD.

The world and humanity which is before us, questions and disturbs us. We would like to be able to discover them in all their dimensions, their 'beyond'. But our gaze only sees the surface of things & of people. We need another kind of sight in order to penetrate more deeply & see as God sees. Only the 'eyes of faith' that's to say the eyes of Jesus Christ grafted onto our human eyes, can give us his Light and equip us for this long pilgrimage.

We will see then, little by little, throughout the history of mankind, even in its smallest details, the spirit of Jesus at work, and his amazing body which is born, develops, dies and is resurrected every day. We will no longer behold simply "Jesus of Nazareth" but Christ unfolding in time his mystery of Creation, of the Incarnation and of Redemption, and we will be able to be with him through our whole life and that of our brothers & sisters & work with him to bring about his Father's Kingdom.

Lord
I would like you to give me enormous eyes
    to look at the world
For I look, Lord.
I like to look,
    but my eyes are small
    too small
to see *beyond* things,
    beyond men and women and events.

I look and guess at life,
    but I only see its hard shell,
    sometimes hard & cruel.
Love signs to me
    but I can only see
    a few of its flowers and fruits,

while the essence escapes me.
And I suffer behind my thick screen,
    I dash myself against its limits
    and sometimes cruelly wound myself,
then a mist rises from my heart
    which darkens my path.
Why, Lord, have you given us eyes
which cannot *see*,
see your *life*, beyond this life
your *love* beyond our love.

Sometimes I believe I can make out ... a few gleams,
    and mysteriously,
    there are born in my heart
    some words a little more beautiful
    than ordinary words,
words which dance in joyous abandon
trying to escape their golden cage.
    They fly from my lips, and I try to capture them,
to make them tell me, so that I can tell
what I divine
surmise
get near
without being able to grasp it.
But in their turn words are like birds that are too small
and I don't wish them to know
how to sing, for me and for the rest of us,
the song of the infinite.

Then, from time to time, I accept,
shutting my eyes for a long time,
and in the depth of my darkness
    I catch a glimpse of
a little of that Light
that the day obstinately hides from me.
    I *see* without seeing,

I *believe.*
But you have given me eyes, Lord,
to see my brothers and sisters,
    legs to go towards them
    and tramp the firm earth with them.
Lord, can I walk with my eyes closed
refusing the light?
    I want to *see* when I look,
but my eyes are small,
    too small
    to behold the beyond.
Lord, give me enormous eyes
    to look at the world.

    Open my eyes, Lord,
    so that I can *see* ...
further than the light of the rising sun,
which suddenly colours nature
with the soft clearness of a young girl's face,
further than the light of the setting sun
where dark patches sketch in
    the shadows of the wrinkles of the earth
like the years on a sunburnt face ...
    so that I can at last *see*
    some reflections of your infinite *light.*

    Open my eyes Lord,
so that I can *see*
beyond the glowing rose and her silent smile,
beyond the hand which passes it to me,
and the heart beyond the hand
and friendship way beyond the heart
... so that I can at last *see*
some reflected gleams of your tenderness.

Open my eyes Lord
   so that I can *see*
   beyond the bodies of the people who attract
or repel me,
beyond their eyes and their gaze
which are set alight or extinguished,
hearts which suffer or rejoice.
I want to see further than the hearts of the flesh,
the blooms of love,
even further than the crazy growths
which are so quickly called sins,
so that I may *see* at last
the children of the good God,
who are born and slowly grow
under the loving gaze of Our Father.

   Open my eyes Lord,
   so that I may see ...
further than the industrial areas,
   at night,
where a thousand flames escape from the hot factories,
further than the volumes of smoke
   which quiver in the wind,
   above the chimneys
   rising to the inaccessible sky,
beyond those disturbing beauties,
   the 20th century towns,
where man ceaselessly refashions the face of the earth,
   ...that I may *see* at last and *hear*,
the heartbeats of thousands of workers
who with are the creators.

   Open my eyes Lord
so that I may *see* ...
beyond the inextricable entanglement
of the numberless human routes,

motorways or roads with no exit,
    red lights
    green lights,
    one way streets and speed limits
roads from the West, the North, or the South
    roads leading to Rome,
or to Mecca,
beyond the thousands of people who have travelled them
for thousands of years
and further than this prodigious mystery of their freedom,
    which throws them,
    thinking
    loving,
    on to these paths in life
    in which their destiny is interwoven,
    ... that I may *see*
    your Calvary raised up,
dominating the World at the Central Crossroads,
    and *you*,
    descended from the cross,
risen from the dead, passing along all these roads of Emmaus,
where so many people go with you without recognition,
    some only on hearing your Word,
    and the breaking of the bread.
That I may *see* at last
    your great Body grow,
    under the breath of the Spirit
    and the maternal labours of Mary
    until the day when you will come to the Father,
    at the end of time
    when O my great Jesus
    you will have reached your state of fullness.

But I know, Lord, that in this world,
I must see without *seeing*

and that on this earth I shall always be
a pilgrim striving to the unknown with the heart unsatisfied.
    I know too that only tomorrow
    passing through the dark gates of the night
    and *seeing you* at last as you are,
    in your own light
    I shall *see* as you see.   *John 1 /3*

I must wait still longer, and walk in the half light ...
but if you wish it, Lord,
    so that my prayer
    with many friends here
    who will share it,
may not be an airy light word of moonshine,
    I beseech you,
    I implore you,
    give us enormous eyes
    to look at the world,
    and we will catch a glimpse of a little of the beyond
and of the people who look at us
    and we will see that we *see*
and then, we shall perhaps be able to say to them at last:
    This *is he Jesus Christ*
    The Light of the World.

The healing of the blind man at Bethsaida.   *Mark 8 vv 22-25*

Living in the truth ... we will grow.   *Ephesians 4 vv 15-16*

For as the body is one whether we are bond or free.
                       Corinthians. 12 vv 12-13

V
Monday Washing.

Jesus travelling through Palestine saw life. Above all the life of the simple people: women making bread, & the one looking for the lost money; the wounded man attacked on the road, the children playing in the square, the widow weeping; the sower of seed in the field, the good harvest and the shepherd with his flock . . .

He looked, he admired. He already saw how all through these lives the seeds of the Kingdom were growing..

Jesus Christ continues to travel our human paths today: "I shall be with you to the end of time . . ." He is present where you can see the smallest gesture of true love: "All love comes from God" (John 1 vv4-7). It is for us to follow him by the signs in those thousands of small things which make up a fertile existence, if they are nourished by this love.

Lord,
   today it is Monday.
      and on balconies,
   here and there, in the concrete yards
      the many coloured mosaic,
   brilliant against the grey background
   the linen drying.

      The many coloured clothes sang like notes in the wind
   and I heard in my heart's ear
      the song of toil
      and the song of love.

    Dirty linen,
    washed linen,
    dried linen,

linen ironed and dirtied once again,
only to be rewashed
redried
reironed,
linen for my husband,
linen for my son
linen for my daughter
and my own in between the two.

Linen from one week to the next,
from washing day to washing day,
from drying to drying,
from ironing to ironing again.

Lord
I offer you this evening,
for all those who do not know you,
or for all those who don't think of praying to you,
This linen, so white
so soft
so supple.
This linen which smells with the goodness of a mother's love,
and the love of married people.

I offer you all these daily tasks
which, repeated a thousand times,
weave beautiful lives in the shadows,
Marvellous lives of the humble,
who know that to live is to carry on
far beyond fatigue.

My child have I not said?
I say it to you
and say it to your brothers:

The Kingdom of Heaven is like a woman,
who during her whole life,
makes dirty linen clean,
not by the power of miraculous washing powder
but by the miracle of love,
given every day.

The Kingdom of God resembles a mustard seed …

Matthew 13 vv 31–35

What shall I do to inherit eternal life?   *Luke 10 vv 25-27*

VI
It would be so easy, Lord.

*Many people who are fighters are tired. They have been grappling with so
many difficulties and misunderstandings that they long to take a back seat, to
rest.*

*Young people, on the other hand, declare they won't repeat what their fathers
have done. They want to use the time to live for themselves. Finally, some
"committed ones" in the world even think that maybe they have deceived
themselves along he way, that they should have prayed more and ... "left the
work to God".*

*This is serious. Very serious. God hasn't given us mankind, humanity, a
world ready made, but to create it ourselves. There is no pretext for a Christian
to retire into his tent and refuse this task. More than others he must, according
to his abilities, consecrate himself to it. This is the absolute criterion for the
authenticity of his love for his brothers and sisters.*

*To have a living faith is not to evade the shop-floor in order to ask God to
take over our work, but to engage ourselves in it with all our strength, while
asking Him to work with us.*

It would be so easy, Lord
to abandon the struggle for a better world ...
    This world which hasn't finished being born.
    It would be so easy
to give up exhausting meetings,
    discussions,
    accounts
those innumerable activities and *involvements*
    that one calls essential,
and of which, on some evenings of extreme fatigue,
    I doubt more and more
    their usefulness to my brothers and sisters.

It would be so easy
to listen to those voices around me,
voices apparently good, friendly,
    even affectionate,
voices which tell me
    'you busy yourself'
    'you batter yourself in vain'
    'you are missing the essential'
voices which insidiously behind my back say
    'he likes doing all this'
    'its his temperament'
    'he cant let go'

    It would be so easy
to give in to discouragement
and to dress it up in good pious intentions,
    about forgotten tasks
    and lack of faith.

    It would then be so easy,
to retire into my house,
to regain my free evenings
and availability at week ends,
    the children's laughter,
    and my wife's embraces.

It would be so easy to sit down,
lick my wounds after the tough battles,
    to rest my legs,
    my arms, my head,
    and my heart, all worn out,
to be in peace far from the hullabaloo of the fights
to hear at last the silence,
    where, far from the noise so they say,

you speak to the *faithful*.
It would be easier Lord,
to stay on the brink, and not jump at all,
to watch others fighting and struggling,
to advise and pity them,
and judge them… and pray for them.
It would be easier.

But Lord,
Is this really what you are asking of me?
    I don't know any more.
    I don't know any more.
    Lord enlighten me help me,
    I don't know any more.

But among the many voices which beset me
    the wise ones,
    the friends
    and those of my loved ones,
I often hear another voice,
    grave and more profound,
    which challenges me, relentlessly
    in my troubled heart:
'You are taking the Lord's place.
Only he can change men and the world.
    Give yourself up to him,
    and he will do what you,
    in your wretched pride,
    believe you can do yourself'.

This voice, Lord, is it yours?
    I don't know any more.
    I don't know any more.
    … But if you really wish it, this evening,

I will resign myself into your hands.
I refuse your resignation my child says the Lord.
    Don't listen to your voices,
      they are not Mine.
    I will never take your place,
      for it is I who have given it to you.
Nothing will happen without you and without
your brothers & sisters,
for I willed you be responsible together,
    both for men and for the world.
But nothing will be done without me ...
and perhaps this
is what you have sometimes forgotten.

Go now, sleep in peace my child
    and tomorrow,
    You and I
    I and you,
    together
    in brotherhood with your brothers and sisters
    will set out again in combat.

Your mother and brothers are outside Who is my mother?

Mark 3 vv 31-35

It is not by saying Lord, Lord.

Matthew 7 vv 21

VII
LORD, WILL YOU COME SHOPPING WITH ME?

Jesus Christ waits for us faithfully, at the heart of our life. But we too often have the impression that in order to pray to him we must stop, cease all activity, in order to be completely with him. Certainly we should do this at certain times. To be there for someone, without even doing anything for him, or with him, but simply offering him the gift of 10 minutes, a quarter of an hour of our life, for free, is the summit of love. But we should also accompany Jesus in the world's highways. Our whole life could become prayer if we thought that he came among us, not to be set apart from us habitually, but to mingle with the very substance of our life and that of our brothers, and to make it grow.

Lord, will you come shopping with me?
It happened that I had to go out shopping
    yet another time;
    I regretted the time spent
    that I believed was wasted.
O this tyrannical time,
    this imposed partner,
implacable companion of my days and years,
    which fragments my life
    pressurises and bosses me about,
    obliging me to run,
    while it runs away so quickly itself!
Am I not its slave?

But this morning, you signalled to me, Lord,
    reminding me that you are there,
    immoveable,
    peaceful,

still.
So I decided to master time,
    to take my time,
abandoning the car and going on foot.
And I said to you, Lord:
'Will you come shopping with me?'

We did it together,
and this evening I want to thank you for coming,
    for I saw things which, without you,
      I wouldn't even have glimpsed.
I saw life in full flood
    in my local streets,
    cars bowling along
    impatient drivers,
    people in a hurry,
    and others strolling.
I saw an angry mother
    dragging along her crying child,
    and another one who
    stopped for a few moments
    to smile and talk to her baby,
an unemployed person begging,
and a lady walking her sweet little dog,
    young people embracing,
and little boys shouting and fighting
    as they came out of school.
I saw the shop fronts,
    welcoming,
    enticing,
and the longing looks at the windows,
caressing a thousand objects of earthly paradise,
advertisements proclaiming the pleasures of life,
    and others which announce the struggle

of those who want to survive.
And I said to you, Lord,
look, Lord,
    you see this person,
    you see that one,
tell them that you love them,
    O yes tell them,
those who live without thinking that you accompany them,
    step by step,
    every day.
And you lent me your eyes, Lord,
and I saw them a little as you do.
    as you see them.

I saw their joys and their sorrows
    behind their expressions
    and the thump of their footsteps,
I saw your Life in their life,
    your Love in their loves,
    in spite of their ignorance
    and perhaps, even their denial.
I saw them, brothers and sisters called by you
to say together, one day:
'Our Father who art in heaven'.
At certain moments
    I no longer thought that you were there...
It's not my fault, Lord,
you are so often silent!
You know that I reproach you for it,
    and that I suffer for it
    so very much!

But now, happily,
I am sure that the strongest love

is not the noisiest.
And *I believe in your love.*
I came back happy,
I had defeated time,
I hadn't wasted my time.
And you were happy,
    you also,
    I am sure of it.
For great spirits tell us, Lord,
    that to pray to you it is necessary
    to stop,
    to be alone,
    to kneel or stand,
    arms so, hands thus,
to shut the eyes to see you better,
the ears to hear you better,
    and begin by...
    and continue by...
    and finish by...
But they forgot to say, Lord,
that it is necessary to go out from time to time,
to go shopping with you,
    and look at the world,
    and look at mankind,
    and look at life,
to gather the joys of all people
    and their secret griefs,
and to give them to you to carry,
you who long to carry the heaviest burdens,
    while for us
    you keep the lightest loads.

O Lord,
    you who gave back to the blind their sight,

and hearing to the deaf,
I beseech you, once more,
    open my eyes,
    open my ears,
I am so often tempted to close them on myself
and when I go out to do my shopping for my body
with you,
    I shall do my shopping for my heart,
and coming back I shall be rich,
    not with what I've bought
    but with what I've seen,
    gathered,
    carried away.
In the evening I shall open my bag before our Father
    to offer him my purchases from life.
And forgive me, Lord
    if I uncover some spoiled fruits,
    which in passing I grabbed for myself,
    thinking them edible.
I will give them to you
    and you will burn them up in your Love.

Jesus went about the towns and villages.   *Matthew 9 vv 35-36*

…'I am the Light of the world'…   *John 8 v 12*

VIII
I AM CARRYING TOO HEAVY A LOAD, LORD, I CAN'T GO ON.

The back-pack of our heart is often full of painful memories, sufferings, and of sins, that we have acquired on our journey through our life and that we carry with us - small pains or great trials, sometimes even heavy secrets that we believe we have shut away for ever.

We try to forget by virtue of: 'one mustn't live in the past!', or to give ourselves peace: 'I don't want to think about it any more!' We push them out. Nonetheless, everything we have lived through lives on in us, and will continue to live, even if our efforts have succeeded in repressing our memories into the unconscious. The life which is repressed rots us, works on our behaviour and even makes us ill. Christians are like children who want to carry burdens on their own which they can hardly lift. The child's father accompanies him, walking at his side. But the child refuses the help which is offered to him. He struggles, suffers, sometimes falls and really hurts himself.

Our father is God. Through his son Jesus Christ he has come to bear our sufferings our sins... But it is necessary to give them to him. And to give them we must not first forget them but have the courage to disinter them, to look them in the face, and accept them. It's at this price that we shall be free and live our life through the risen Lord.

I am carrying too much, Lord,
    I can't go on!
But this evening I believe I have at last found
    what, for a long time,
      you were expecting me to find.
My life's journey is not very long, Lord,
    but my past is laden.
I have had so many blows in my daily life
    and lived through so many events,
      which have hurt me,
      disturbed me,

and have marked me with indelible regret;
I have tried every thing
in vain.

I have been told, Lord
that small sufferings go away quickly
 and that large pains
 are wiped away with time.
That one must be brave and not think about it any more,
for the past is past and must be forgotten.
 And I have struggled, as you know.
Countless times I have tried to turn the page
 so as not to look at it any more,
but with a puff of wind
the album of photographs of my old memories
is reopened every time.

I have tried to excise my wounds,
 with a thousand soothing counsels
 beautiful ideas,
 beautiful feelings,
and even great surges of faith and repeated prayers.
 But at the least of life's blows,
 the sores are reopened,
 and bleed.
One has to start again.
For a time I believed I had managed.
Proudly I said: 'It is done',
 for I have accepted everything and don't think of it any more.
But the memories and buried sufferings
 were still alive in me.
 Like wild plants
 their roots live on,
 and when I try to tear off
 their leaves and fruit
they grow again vigorously

in the field of my heart.
    My tears water them.
    They develop.
    They invade me,
    smother me,
    eat up my life,
    leave me depressed,
and penetrate between the very stones
of my foundations,
thick walls
that I believed solid
but which brutally
collapse in whole sections.

And nevertheless, Lord,
sometimes I believe I am liberated.
I have no more sad memories…!
    I can sleep at last.
But alas, in the night
I am violently disturbed,
    for the ghosts of those memories
    emerge from their hiding places,
    and disguised in a thousand mad ways
    in my dreams or nightmares,
    dance their farandoles.
    I wake up tired ,drained.

The load is too heavy for me, Lord,
    I cannot go on.
But this evening…
Was I dreaming, Lord?
    I believed that I had at last found
what you had wanted from me for a long time.
For, by chance, I read
    a sentence from a psalm
    printed on a holy image:

'Cast thy burden upon the Lord
    and he will sustain you'   *Psalm 55 v 22*
    And I believe that through these words
    you spoke to me.
O Lord forgive me
    for all that lost time
    for the thousand sufferings,
    and so many discouragements,
for my dismal complaints,
    and those mad revolts
    in my blinkered life,
    suppressed,
    wasting my life,
which festered in my heart,
manured by rotten weeds.

O Lord forgive me, for you were there.
You were waiting for me to come with me
    ...and carry the heaviest load,
like a father who helps his little child,
and only leaves in his hands
    just what he can carry by himself.
But I didn't see you
    because I only saw my sufferings.
I didn't hear you
    because I was listening to the sound of my sorrow,
and alone,
proud,
    I wanted to keep everything to myself.
O Lord forgive me, because you were there,
you were waiting to take me in your arms
    to raise me up,
    to carry me,
at the same time as carrying my load.
But Lord it was necessary,
finally to accept all that I have lived through.

I give it to you freely,
for you do not take by force
what is not freely given.
Here I am at last,
before you, Lord,
   at my last gasp,
    at the end of my life.
I want to give you *everything.*
...but without you, Lord,
   I know
   I will not be able to manage it.

Help me Lord, I beseech you,
for I will need a lot of time
to uproot everything,
   but without damaging anything.
It will take many efforts to remove everything bad
   without disturbing what, in spite of everything,
   I would like to keep.
A lot of humility is needed to reveal all
   that I would like to hide.
I will need a lot of time
in order to get used to giving to you each day
all the small and all the heavy stones on my journey,
   those on which I stumble,
   those which are sent me
   through carelessness or malice,
   those which I throw at other people,
   and which rebound on me.
Help me, Lord,
with the difficulties of my life,
   of yesterday
   and of today.
   Help me to look without fear,
   rather than turning away my eyes.
To dig up

rather than to bury,
to dare to remember
rather than trying to forget,
and even, to feel, and feel anew, what I have undergone
rather than to suppress it.
For I will only be able to give you
what I consent to,
what I hold in my trembling hands,
what you,
you for ever wait to liberate me from.

The load was too heavy for me, Lord,
I couldn't go on...
But you have invited me
to empty my heart's back-pack each evening.
Then I will be
like the little child in his father's arms,
in his mother's arms,
who has told all his troubles
and who goes to sleep in peace,
because he knows that he is loved
and that his parent's love
is stronger than anything.

Cast your cares on the Lord	*Psalm 55 v 22*
Into your hands O Lord I commit my spirit	*Psalm 30*
Come unto me all ye that travail...	*Matthew 2 vv 28-29*
I am speechless...	*Psalm 31*
I will lay me down in peace...	*Psalm 4*

IX
My God, I do not believe.

Many sincere, but ignorant or naïve believers have caricatured the face of God. People around us reject the caricature more and more. They are right. It is false. But for us, who is God? He who is all-powerful in human terms or he who is all powerful Love?

In the first case, and on the pretext of faith, we risk disengaging ourselves. It is God who does everything – leave it to him!. More seriously we risk constructing, little by little, a religion of servitude and of fear. One must win the good favour of God, obey in order to avoid punishment and above all everlasting torment. Even more seriously, we draw God into insoluble issues making him responsible for or in collusion with unjust deaths and all kinds of suffering which crush humanity.

In the second case, we try step by step, to live our life as a loving response to Love, which is for ever offered but never imposed. Then, marvelling, we discover to what extent we are free before God, responsible for our lives, and for those of our brothers and sisters and of the world..

The essence of faith is to believe that we are infinitely loved. If we accept this Love, then our behaviour changes completely. We are reborn and from slaves become free children of an adored Father. And from love and not from duty we try to fulfil all that our Father wishes.

My God, I do not believe
that you make the rain to fall or the sun to shine
by free choice,
on demand,
so that the Christian peasant's corn ripens
or that the harvest festival is a success.
That you find work for the 'right minded' unemployed
and leave the rest to look
and never find it.

That you keep safe
the child whose mother has prayed,
    and let the little one be killed
    who has no mother to pray to you.
That you yourself feed the people,
    when we ask you to,
    and leave them to die of hunger
    when we stop asking.

    My God, I do not believe,
that you are leading us where you want
    and that we have only to allow ourselves to be led.
That you send us this trial
    and that we have only to submit to it.
That you offer us this success
    and that we have only to thank you for it.
That when you finally decide to summon to yourself
    the one we love,
    we have only to resign ourselves.

No, my God, I do not believe
that you are a dictator
    possessing all powers,
    imposing your will
    for the good of your people.
That we are marionettes,
    whose strings you pull
    at a whim
and that you are manipulating a mysterious scenario,
    whose smallest details of stage management
    you fixed from the first.
No, I do not believe it.
    I don't believe it any more,
because I know, O my God,
    that you do not want it

and that you cannot want it,
because you are *Love*,
because you are *Father*,
    and we are your children.

    O my God, forgive me,
because for too long we have disfigured your adorable face.
We believed that to know you
and understand you
it was necessary to imagine you
    encompassed for ever
    with power and might.
In our human manner we dreamt of you too often like this.
We have used exact words
    to think of you and talk of you,
and in our constricted hearts these words have imprisoned you.
    And we have translated
    all might,
    will,
    commandment,
    obedience,
    judgement...
into our proud human language.
And have dreamed of dominating our brothers and sisters.
Then we have attributed to you
    punishments,
    sufferings and deaths,
    while all you have wanted for us
    is forgiveness,
    happiness and life.

O my God, yes, forgiveness,
for we have not dared to believe, that by love,
    you have, since eternity, wanted us *free*,
not only free to say yes or no

to what you have decided for us in advance,
but free to reflect,
to choose,
act,
at every moment of our life.

We have not dared to believe
that you have so longed for this freedom
that you have risked sin,
evil,
suffering,
the distorted outcome of our misguided freedom,
the horrible suffering of your derided love.
That you have even risked losing,
in the eyes of many of your children,
your halo of infinite goodness
and the glory of your omnipotence.

We have not dared to understand, finally,
that when you wanted to reveal yourself to us definitively,
you came to this earth
small,
weak,
naked.
And that you died on the cross
abandoned,
'powerless',
naked.
To show to the world that your only power,
is the infinite power of Love,
love which frees us
so that we can love.
O my God, now I know that you do everything
except take away our freedom!

Thank you, my God, for this beautiful and terrifying freedom,
  supreme gift of your infinite love.
  We are free!
  Free!
Free to conquer, little by little, nature,
  to put it to the service of our brothers and sisters,
or free to alter nature
  exploiting it for our benefit alone.
Free to defend and develop life,
  to fight against all suffering
  and all sickness,
or free to squander intelligence, energy, money,
  to make arms
  and kill each other.
Free to give you children or refuse you them,
to organize ourselves and share our wealth,
or leave millions of people
dying of hunger on this fertile earth.
Free to love
  or free to hate.
Free to follow you
  Or reject you.

We are free
  but loved *infinitely*.

And so, my God, I believe
that because you love us and are our Father,
since eternity you have dreamed for us eternal happiness
  that you unceasingly offer us
  but never impose on us.
I believe that your loving Spirit
  is the heart of our life,
  and inspires in us every day without fail

the wishes of your Father.

And I believe that in the middle of the vast entanglement
    of human liberties,
    the events which happen to us,
    the ones we chose,
    and those we didn't choose,
    whether they were good or bad,
source of joy or of cruel suffering,
    can all,
thanks to your Spirit which accompanies us,
thanks to you whom we love in your Son,
thanks to our freedom opening itself to your love,
    all become through us and for us,
    part of our way to you.

O my great and loving God,
    so humble and self effacing,
    that I can never realise and understand you
    unless I am a child again,
grant that I shall believe with all my strength
    your sole omnipotence,
    the omnipotence of your love.
Then I will one day, gathered together with my brothers and sisters,
proud of having remained a free person,
    overflowing with happiness,
    hear you say,
'Go my child, your faith has saved you!'

He chose us in Christ, before the world was created.

Ephesians 1 vv 4-6

He who does not love has not known God.   *1 John 4 vv 8-10*

X
My friend died last night, Lord.

All creatures are born, live and die. So has God willed. But we should all die a natural death at the end of our life. Premature deaths, from accident or illness are not the act of God, of his will, any more than that of chance.

Accidents are for the most part the sad consequences of our freedom. Only through the light of God will we discover what part is our responsibility, and that of our fellow beings, in the vast confusion of our activities. Many accidents would be avoided if we lived as Jesus asked us to live.

Many diseases remain unconquered. They are the outcome of nature which we have not yet mastered.

It is our human task to accomplish this. God, who gave us the earth to conquer and put to the service of humanity trusts us. Apart from rare exceptions, he does not take our place by doing miracles. It is for the researchers, doctors, etc to do battle. But alas, we give ourselves many illnesses by mistreating our bodies and even more our hearts, and too often we devote much more money, brains and energy, to inventing means of killing, than to finding and putting into action means of protecting and developing life.

Happily, God does not leave us alone, he came in Jesus Christ to fight with us. In our fight he offers us the omnipotent strength of his Love, and suffering itself, which is and remains evil, can be, through him, the occasion for added saving love.

My friend died tonight Lord,
at his last breath
at the end of his life
fighting against cancer
till the last moment,
with his family doctor and friends.
I do not say Lord,
'since you so desired it, be it according to thy will',

43

and still less your holy will.
　　But I say to you, very quietly,
very quietly because many, alas,
of those around me would never understand,
I say to you, Lord, my friend is dead,
　　and you could do nothing about it.
Nothing that, stupidly, I was dreaming of.
Nothing that, stupidly, I was hoping for.
　　And I weep.
　　torn apart,
　　bereft,
　　but my heart is at peace,
for I have this morning understood a little more
　　that you were weeping with me.

Yes Lord, I have understood.
　　Thanks to you
　　thanks to my friend,
but help me, I beg you ,to believe it
　　that you do not desire death
　　but life,
　　and that, more than any of us
　　because you love more,
you suffer to see so many of your children
　　dying before their time.

I have understood that except for rare exceptions,
and in this is the mystery of your being,
in the battles waged against illness
　　through respect, through love,
you have never wished to take our place,
　　but always you have offered to suffer
　　and to fight with us.
　　I have understood...

For my friend, Lord,
did not entreat you for a miracle
but asked that his doctor friends should have
    the strength to search
    and to do battle right to the end.
    He besought for himself
    the courage to suffer,
to accept the two operations,
the treatments and the whole experience
so that others after him
should suffer less
and even someday be healed..

He did not ask that his own family
    should have the grace to be *resigned*
    but the grace to protect life,
    to respect it,
    and develop it.
And right to the end, cradled by the music he loved,
    asked that everyone should have...
    the joy of living.

My friend, Lord, did not offer up his suffering,
For suffering he said *is bad,*
And God does not love suffering.
He offered his long and painful fight
    against suffering.
    That prodigious energy
    that strength that emerged from him
    thanks to you, Lord,
that extra love and faith, necessary
    in order not to despair
    but to believe that his life
    is renewed through you,

beyond death.
In the end my friend, Lord,
did not offer his suffering,
but like you,
and with you,
O my Saviour Jesus,
he gave his life, so that we,
we should live.
My friend died tonight Lord,
and I weep,
but my heart is at peace,
for my friend died tonight
but with you
he gave me life.

God said, Let man be made in my image.   *Genesis 1 v 26*

Creation waits, anticipating the revelation of the Son of God.
Romans 8 vv 19-22

Martha said to Jesus, Lord if you had been here.
John 11 vv 21-26

XI

Life is before me, Lord, ...but you are with me.

Many young people are afraid of the future, above all their professional future and their family's. They do not know what routes they will take and where these routes will take them. Some are in such anguish they refuse to grow up in order to avoid choosing.

Fear is unwholesome. It paralyses. Human greatness is in being able to "risk life" - having first reflected thoroughly, but without waiting for 'all risk insurance cover' which is impossible to obtain.

If risk is dangerous, committing oneself consciously and faithfully to Jesus Christ does not take any effort but guarantees peace of mind. He can only want our true happiness and to help us to obtain it whatever the difficulties along the way.

Life is before me, Lord,
    like a seductive fruit
but life often frightens me,
      for to gather the fruits
      it is necessary to go out from home
      and start on the way,
      to walk
      and walk,
but on a road which turns and twists unceasingly
and on which you cannot see ahead
      the places that await you
      or the hidden obstacles,
      the outstretched hands
      or the faces which turn away.

To leave, Lord,
is a thrilling adventure
I want to live …
but I am often afraid.
I am afraid of entering, tomorrow, the immense workshop
where the multitude of the world's builders are employed.
Will I find a place where
so many new hands remain unoccupied
and so many knowledgeable heads
wait to be employed?

I am afraid of the mysterious world
which both fascinates and terrifies me
for I hear the bursts of laughter
and I see the pleasures
which beckon me from afar.
But I also hear
the vast clamour of suffering humanity,
and these cries
that I cannot make silent revolt me.
I am afraid of this love
which in the mornings sings in my heart
and in the depth of the night
I long for with all my being,
the mysterious energy which fills my heart
and overflows into my body,
the besetting urge, as the days lengthen,
to meet a *face* at last,
a face which I will know and which will recognise me
as the sought-for unique one,
the desire to gaze on it caressingly,
gently clasp it in my hands
to taste lips at last and be tasted,

above all the hunger, that one day this love
may be one flesh,
    and there will be the cry,
    the cry of a new life,
    when love bears fruit.

But I long for it and am afraid, Lord,
so many loves have failed under my eyes,
    illusions of happiness,
    like burst bubbles;
so many loves embarked on
    and ended without accepting the risk,
so many friends, couples,
    who believed themselves joined together for ever
    and who have been so quickly torn apart!

Yes, I am afraid, Lord,
    I dare to admit it to myself
    and I dare to tell you,
but if I shut my eyes today,
it is not to refuse
to *see* the way before me,
    but to find you again, to pray to you,
    for I long to live, Lord,
    I long
And I trust in you.

    O my God,
may I never forget to give you thanks for life,
    for life is yours,
    you who are Father
    and Father of all life,
you have made me your son,
    your son born for joy.

Make me proud to be human,
    complete as you want me to be,
accepting from you this marvellous vocation
        to make myself a person
        to raise myself, to grow
in order to set off rich and free,
        on this road before me.
Let me welcome life
        with all my heart,
        with all my strength,
since my parents through love have given it to me,
        even if love,
        perhaps,
        is fragile,
but I am responsible for my life,
        since they have given it to me.

Help me never to fritter away my life,
        the life of my body which is misused
        and of a soul which loses its way.
Help me never to steal the life of others,
        but just accept it when it is offered,
to resist shutting it away in an enclosed heart,
        instead of offering
        my brothers and sisters in need,
        so much that I haven't shared with them.

Give me the desire always to seek you,
        to meet you, know you and love you
        and with you become the friend you want,
accepting your life into my life,
        so that my fruits and flowers
        are yours
        simultaneously with mine.

Help me to walk
>without wanting to know
>what the way has in store for me
>at every turn,
not head in the clouds,
>but feet on the ground
>and my hand in your hand.
Then Lord I shall leave home
>confident and rejoicing
And without fear will set off on the unknown way,
>for life is before me,
But you are walking with me.

Wherefore if God so clothe the grass which today is ...
Matthew 6 vv 30–34

Jesus got into the boat. His disciples followed. There arose a great
storm. *Matthew 8 vv 23–26*

XII

LORD, IT WAS YOU, THAT UNEMPLOYED PERSON WHOM I MET AN HOUR AGO.

2000 years ago Jesus of Nazareth was betrayed, arrested, unjustly condemned, tortured, executed. Dying on the cross he took on himself all our sins, all our sufferings. His historic passion was accomplished. But through its members it continues to unfold today.

Jesus Christ continues to suffer through every person who suffers. In that sense one can say that his Way of the Cross is not finished.

Jesus died a victim of our sins. It is because of them that he was crucified. God does not punish us for our faults. It is we who punish ourselves, individually and collectively. This goes on being repeated.

The great scourges like the under development of peoples and the endless atrocious suffering it causes them wars, unemployment, etc are all, in different ways, fruits of the collective sins of humanity.

God does not change stones into bread but he has given us his Word. Strengthened by this Word we must help the victims of sin, but also fight with our brothers and sisters and our Brother, to destroy the causes of so many and so many sufferings.

Lord,
    You must be tired this evening,
because you queued for a long time
at the employment office.
    You must be humiliated this evening,
because today you heard
so many wounding comments.
    You must be discouraged this evening,
because tomorrow...
    you will have come to *the end of your rights*.

The end of the right to eat.
The end of the right to feed your family.
The end of the right to live...
And you will only have the right to die.

Lord,
    how you must suffer this evening!
For it was you, that unemployed person,
that I met an hour ago.
It was you,
    I know it,
because you told me in your Holy Gospel
    I was naked,
    a stranger,
    ill,
    a prisoner...
    an unemployed person!
It was you, I know it.
But I didn't think about it any more.

Lord,
So your Way of the Cross is that long!
    I who believed it was ended.
    I who believed you had finally reached the end
    high up there on Golgotha
    at the end of long hours of torture,
    after a life of 30 odd years.

I knew that you came to us
    like us,
    one of us,
and that we saw you take to the road with us,

faithfully taking your place
in the long line of suffering people.
    But I didn't know
    that your Way of the Cross was begun
    long ago,
    at the beginning of time
    when the first men and women,
      on the first lands.
first endured suffering.
And I didn't know that it would not be ended,
until the last men and women
had cried out for the last time
    on the last crosses.

For 2000 years ago, Lord,
you played your part to the end
    faithfully,
    perfectly.
The way of the cross of your brothers and sisters is long,
    very long
    and you have not stopped being with them, beside them,
    exploited,
    rejected,
    humiliated,
    imprisoned,
    stripped,
    tortured,
    crucified,
body and soul blazing forth
proclaiming at one time your supreme suffering
on all the crosses in the world,
crosses erected by mankind.

You have taught me now, Lord!
That the one who loves
suffers the suffering of the beloved.
And the more he loves, the more he suffers,
    And you who are infinitely loving
Suffer infinitely to see us suffering.
    So it is
That entering perfectly into all our pain
    you are the Lord,
    crucified through your members
    till the end of time.
And that is your Great Passion
of suffering and of love.

    Lord,
I was not on the path to Golgotha,
    2,000 years ago,
like your mother who wept
but in her sorrow offered you.
Like the holy women who wailed,
the ones in the crowd who were silent from fear,
the ones who shouted from hatred,
and like Simon of Cyrene who served you
    from duty.
But today I am there and I see you
    when I see the suffering people,
    and I talk to you when I talk to them,
and I help you to carry your cross
when I help them carry theirs.

    O Lord,
    I would like to be
Simon of Cyrene on humanity's way of the cross.
For what good is it to shed tears for you

who died 2,000 years ago,
    if I do not suffer with my brothers and sisters
    who suffer today?
For what use is it to meditate
    and groan in pious ceremonies
    if I do not see you every day
    grieving on my way?

    But this evening, praying,
    before them,
    before you,
I also thought, Lord, that the crosses of men and women
do not just happen.
We make them ourselves,
    every day alas,
    through our egoisms,
    our pride
and the long catalogue of our many sins.

We are *constructors of the cross!*
    Working at our accounts
or together
    in well organised industries.
    producing crosses on the production line
    which are more and more numerous
    more and more perfected.
    crosses for disrupted homes,
    crosses for children abandoned,
    crosses for people dying of hunger,
    crosses for soldiers on the battlefield,
    crosses for ...unemployed people.
    And crosses...
and crosses...
always crosses

in all shapes and sizes!
And if, Lord, we must be Simon of Cyrene
        for our suffering brothers and sisters,
we must
        fight together
to dismantle our innumerable factories of crosses.

        Thank you, Lord,
for you
were that person
that I met an hour ago.
And it is you,
who through him,
today, has spoken to me once more.

When the Son of man shall come into his glory ... For I was hungry ...
Matthew 25 vv 31-40

Always bearing about in the body the dying of the Lord Jesus, That
the life also of Jesus might be made manifest in our body.
2 Corinthians vv 4-10

Bear ye one another's burdens and so fulfil the law of Christ.
Galatians 6 v 2

XIII
Prayer in the depth of my solitude.

God is 'continuing relationship', Father, Son, Holy Spirit, united in such
a way that they are one. Man is 'made in the image of God'; he is also a
'relation' but not complete and perfect. He has to make himself and advance
in relationship through knowledge, respect and love for all men, and above all
for those near him.
Now, one of the most important and dramatic features of the modern world is
the breakdown of links between people. They bury themselves in towns, their
homes and cars, but often pass each other by without meeting in depth.
Hence the solitude of many among them, and more particularly old people,
the ill, the handicapped, and prisoners... It is very serious, for people without
relationships come apart, slowly destroy themselves, and can die of solitude.
The person who waits for someone to join him or her 'in the depth of solitude'
sometimes risks a long wait. If he or she wants to overcome it, let him or her
go out and approach other people. Jesus Christ will accompany him or her, he
who came to make the human race one body in him.

I am alone.
Alone Lord, do you understand?
   Alone.
   And outside there is a holiday.

I have turned off my radio,
which so often apes being a companion for me
   but silence has abruptly
   entered the room,
and anguish
   has crept into my heart.
At one moment I thought I heard
   some noises on the staircase,
I imagined footsteps...

someone coming up?
>Why this mad hope
>since I expect no one,
>...and that no one will come!

If you wanted, Lord,
you would send me someone!
>I need someone,
I need a hand, Lord,
>no more than a hand in my hand
>like a bird perched there.
I need lips on my forehead, the warmth of a kiss.
I need a look
>one direct look,
>to prove
that at least I exist for someone.
I need a few words in fact,
>and through these words a beating heart offered to me.
>But no one will come.
>I am alone.
>Alone.
>And outside it's a holiday.

Yes, you can speak Lord,
at the bottom of my heart I can hear!
But I know your song,
>the one that the clergy tell me:
'You are not alone, since I am there.'
Yes you are there
>but without hands,
>without lips,
>without eyes and without words.
And I am not an angel,
>since you have given me flesh.
You won't say any more to me Lord?
>Not you either!

You angry?
I have lived in my prison of solitude for a long time,
 and my jumbled words,
  stuck to the grille,
  couldn't find the door
  through which I might escape,
undeserved prisoner that I am.

 But suddenly I think,
unless its you speaking to me anew,
 I think that others besides me,
 languish in solitude.
 I know some of them nearby,
 and know the hard world,
where millions of people,
bodies piled on bodies,
in housing estates or in crowds,
 pass one another by,
 rub up against one another,
 bump into each other,
 without ever meeting.
This is not what you wanted Lord,
you said that you came
to gather your scattered children together,
 and by giving your life
 to make them a single family.

Now my suffering, Lord,
tells me at length about the sufferings of others,
and I hear their complaints,
more strongly than my own.
And at last I understand,
 that there is only one remedy
 to cure my solitude,
 which is to go out to other people
 to heal theirs.

I have found my vocation Lord!
I, who so often feel myself to be cruelly useless,
    and capable of so little,
    in spite of a big heart,
I shall be part of the Church, a maintenance worker
I shall try to strengthen the ties that have been loosened,
    and perhaps I shall repair
    those that have been broken.
In this way I shall mend the fabric of the family a little,
for since you, Lord, no longer have, on this earth,
    hands, lips,
    eyes and words,
I offer myself as subcontractor,
    for all those who like me,
    need a person,
    even an ageing person,
to tell them that they are not alone
and that Someone loves them.

    Goodbye solitude!
It is late tonight, but tomorrow Lord,
    I promise you,
I will begin my work
and go and see my neighbour.
    Goodnight Lord...
    And since, once again,
    being deprived of kisses,
    I had none to give
Tomorrow I will have one all ready to give.

Jesus came to the place called Gethsemane.   *Matthew 26 vv 36-40*

Well beloved, if God has so loved us.   *John 4 vv 11-12*

XIV
Life is beautiful Lord, and today it is Easter.

Jesus said to his disciples that they must take up their cross and follow him. But we must follow him right to the end. Now Jesus did not stop at Golgotha nor in the tomb. We believe that he is ALIVE, resurrected. Drawn along with him in his death - our death to sin - we rise again with him, living a new life, his.

Similarly, in a certain way, the passion of Jesus Christ is not complete, for he continues through his followers to suffer and to die every day. One can say that the resurrection has not reached its fullness. Easter is not only an event in the past - the greatest Event in history - every day is Easter, when we accept in Jesus Christ our Saviour, the "passing from death to sin", to the Life which he offers.

For sure, the whole of the "human climb" does not give automatic entry into the Kingdom, but it is part of the mystery of creation which develops in Christ "for by him were all things created ... all things were created by him and for him: And he is before all things and in him all things subsist".

Humanity grows in Christ; in him it rises again every day and will rise again to the end of time.

Life is beautiful Lord
and I want to gather it,
as one gathers flowers on a spring morning.
But I know Lord
that the flower only grows
at the end of a long winter when death has held sway.

Forgive me Lord,
I do not believe firmly enough in life's spring,
for too often life seems to me a long winter,
which will never cease to mourn

its dead leaves
and its lost flowers.
Although I believe in you Lord,
with all my heart
I knock at your tomb, and I find it empty.

And when today's apostles tell me
that they have seen you alive
I am like Thomas
I need to see and to touch.
Give me enough faith
I beseech you Lord,
to hope for spring in the hardest winter,
and to believe in the triumph of Easter
after the death of Good Friday.

For Lord, you are risen!
You are alive!
our friend and brother
for ever one with us,
you who so loved us
that *you became Man*
leading us with you to death to sin
the true death.
You are our 'head',
first come from the womb of the earth
first man born in heaven,
now you draw forward your brothers and sisters one by one,
the 'members' of your body,
until all humanity reunited at last
is brought by you,
with you,
in you,
into the Holy Trinity.

Lord you are risen!
By your grace triumphant life
    has emerged from the tomb.
Henceforth the source will never dry up
    new life is offered to all,
    to recreate us for ever,
children of a God who awaits us,
for daily Easters
and *eternal joy*

It was Easter yesterday Lord,
    but it is Easter today,
Every time that we accept dying to ourselves,
We with you open a breach
    in the tomb of our hearts,
so that the Source may spring out and your Life may flow.
    And so many many people
    do not know alas,
    that you are there already,
    in their human endeavour.
Later, in your light they will discover it.

It was Easter yesterday,
    but it is Easter today,
when a child shares his sweets,
    having secretly struggled
    not to keep them all for himself.
When a husband and wife embrace again
    after a small tiff or a serious split.
When finally adversaries after a long battle
    sign a really just agreement.
When researchers have found the saving cure
    and the doctor brought a life back
    which would have been extinguished without him.

When the doors of the prison are opened
    and the penalty is paid,
    and when even in the cell the prisoner
    shares cigarettes with his companions.
When, after long efforts, a person
    finds work
    and brings a little earned money home.
When newspapers announce the conference of the great
    has made progress with the world's problems.

    It is Easter every day,
    a thousand thousand Easters,
but I do not know enough Lord,
to look around me
and see the flowers of spring
more than the dead leaves.

This evening I do not want Lord,
when praying to you,
    to lament endlessly over myself,
    weeping over my sins
    and the sins of the world,
    which have all led you to the tomb
    and which have caused our death.
I don't want to delay, imploring forgiveness,
    for all that imprisoning
    and burying
    which too often makes life full of despair.
With you, Lord,
I shall not camp in the Garden of Olives this evening,
    in order to wake up tomorrow with a Good Friday head
For I who am so often irritated
    by the too facile Alleluias,
Shall make my evening prayer

just a profound thanksgiving
  for the stones rolled away,
  for those who have risen from the tomb
  and for this New Life
  which today has sprung up under my feet.
  Yes Lord, life is beautiful,
  for it is your Father who made it.
  Life is beautiful
for it is you who have given it back to us
when we had lost it.
  Life is beautiful
for it is *your very life* offered for us ...
  But we must make it flower
  and I must offer it for you each evening
  and gather it on human byways
as a child on a walk
gathers the flowers of the field
to make a bouquet
to give to his parents.

Life is beautiful, Lord,
it was Easter *today*.

It was the first day of the week... the doors were closed.

John 20 vv 19-20

Christ whom you have received, Jesus the Saviour ...

Colossians 2 vv 6-7 & 9-12

If ye then be risen with Christ.   *Colossians 3 v 1*

XV
IN THE PARIS TRAIN, IN LIFE'S TRAIN.

Where do we come from? Where are we going? Have we embarked on 'the train of life' without knowing at what station we got on and what station awaits us? Alas, so many of our brothers and sisters do not know. And we too we often forget that Jesus Christ is present on the train, with us.
Our journey is never a solitary journey. We are all travelling together. In the Paris train, in a bus, but also in a building, in an office, in a team, as part of an organisation - wherever we are! We can isolate ourselves seeking an artificial tranquillity. We can also open ourselves to others and create links so that life can circulate. We can, in the end, if we have communicated a little with other people, in prayer guide them to Jesus Christ right to the arrival station.

Lord,
It's hot in the train to Paris.
Many passengers doze, some read.
One next to me does crosswords
    and several keep up a noisy exchange
    of words and laughter.
As for me, I look at the countryside.
    It flies past us
    before I've even been able to take it in.,
Just like life.
I dream.

I have carefully chosen to sit where I shall be alone,
    someone near me would inhibit my movements,
    and if they smiled at me I would have to smile,
    and if they spoke to me I would have to reply.

I am there,
    enclosed in my body,
    enclosed in my head,
    enclosed in my heart.
I see the other people, but I don't want to look at them
I hear them, but I don't want to listen to them
I want to be alone.
    Tranquil.

Now I am going to read.
I mustn't waste too much time!
But now you sign to me,
    Lord.
You are here too,
    traveller on all my journeys,
    my discreet companion,
And like a seasoned lover,
    I was once more
    forgetting your silent presence.
You are here, and slowly you open my eyes for me,
    you open my ears.
You wake me gently
    like one wakes a child who wants to sleep more.
You cannot leave me tranquil,
    Lord!
Must one ceaselessly see others,
    hear others,
    think of others?
    And what about me?

Who will think of me if I don't …
    and my book?…
    Ever since I began to read it
    I have wanted to finish it!

It's a good book, Lord,
    It gives me good ideas,
    ideas in my head,
    which turn and return,
    and which nourish my soul,
and good feelings
    which nourish my heart.
I assure you, Lord, that in reading it
    I am not wasting my time...
But I know that I waste it arguing, arguing with You.
It's futile to persist,
    you are always right.

    I have shut the book and open my eyes.
You have won Lord!

...I am not alone any more,
    but I'm not tranquil any more.
My neighbours are there
and my neighbours' neighbours,
those in my compartment,
    in my carriage, and all the others.
They are there, living,
    flesh and bone,
    laughing, talking,
    silent,
    full of joys and sorrows,
    a thousand open books, for me,
and each one has his own chapter...
They are there, embarked on the same train,
    or the same journey,
They roll along together, in the same rhythm,
    together for 2 hours,
    bound for the same destination.

Such is the train,
Such is life.
　　A look,
　　a smile
　　a word,
and I am in touch again with what I didn't want to be in touch with,
and I have connected again with what I didn't want to be connected with.

Now I am with them, Lord,
　　among them,
　　one of them.
I accept them at last
and today present them to you
when I present myself to you,
　　I with them.
And on Sunday I will offer them to you
in your Eucharist,
　　here all trains converge
　　on the station of eternity.

Such is the train,
such is life.

　　But, Lord,
are not my companions themselves also
　　blind and deaf?
Thoughtlessly embarked one day,
　　many of them do not know
　　either the reason or the object of the journey.

　　They roll along
　　in the train of life.
　　I would like to tell them where we're going,
　　I would like to tell them that the route is beautiful,

even if it is difficult,
and that it would be less difficult
if we were together, *united*.
I would like to tell them that we are not alone,
since you want to travel with us,
but that we must get to know you,
recognise you, and follow you,
you who said:
I am the route, the Way.

Rest assured, my child,
says the Lord,
Today *I need you*,
your open eyes,
your open ears,
and your open heart.
I need a *yes*,
even yours alone,
so that you should be reunited
to take command and drive the train,
so that the journey should not be a journey
going nowhere.
It is true, alas, that many travellers,
in the Paris train,
in life's train,
will make the journey without meeting me.
So many tunnels have been built
on mankind's lines,
that they travel in the dark,
without seeing themselves and without seeing me,
and your light, my friends,
my disciples,
is too often hidden to illuminate them.
But since I have come to take the train with them,

since you have at last come to see me
and to see them
and to welcome them
and present them to me,
I tell you, one day in my *Light*
many will know me,
when, having arrived at the station,
dazzled they will exclaim:
'it was there!'
and seeing me will shout
'it was You, with us!'

In the Paris train,
in life's train
I am with them,
but *I need you.*

Jesus said to him 'I am the Way and the Truth...'   *John 14 vv 6-7*

'Father I will that they also ... be with me where I am'.
                                                    John 17 v 24

XVI
MY FRIENDS SAID TO ME: "LETS DRINK A CUP TOGETHER".

People need to meet. Through gestures they try the adventure of encounter.
"Have a drink", is one of these often repeated gestures.
Underneath this quest for friendship is hidden a thirst more profound than the
search for a legitimate but human satisfaction. Mankind needs God and
thirsts for a drink that will refresh the soul. Jesus Christ offers us his 'living
water', his Life, which is shed for us and for our brothers and sisters, till
eternity.
We should go more often to drink at the fountain.

My friends said to me,
   'Will you come and have a drink?'
And I thought, Lord,
   of those endless invitations,
   repeated every day:
'Will you have a drink?
'What would you like?'
'Come along, we are celebrating my birthday!'
'And now ... let's drink a cup together!'
   To drink, and drink again ...
   Lord,
   are people always thirsty?

They are thirsty, I know.
Thirsty in body, perhaps sometimes,
   but above all in the heart.
Lonely people
who seek the company of their brothers and sisters
for conversation,

for gales of laughter to drown their sorrows,
    looks exchanged
    of amusement or complicity,
    gestures which touch them,
so that they know they exist,
and that they are recognised,
and to *feel*
that through this network of connections,
    created for one moment,
    a little life is circulating
    which warms and unites.

They are thirsty.
They invite each other to a drink,
    but their thirst is not quenched.
Tomorrow, they will start again.

I too am thirsty, Lord,
    with the thirst of fragmented life.
But I know that my human thirst
    hides another one,
the thirst for your life in mine.
I search for you, Lord,
but too often I am
far away, too far,
    while you are waiting for me, nearby,
...so near, that I don't see you.
And yet, you said to me,
    "He who keeps my word
    my Father will love him and I will love him,
    and we will come to him,
    and will make our abode with him"   *John 14 23*

Why, Lord,
why then so often,
    do I travel alone in my arid desert
    with parched lips
    and empty hands,
why do I live without life
    when you offer me yours?
Enable me I implore you,
    to hear more often,
    beneath the bustle of my days,
your silent invitations.
For you also, Lord,
    you offer me a drink!
    a drink of Water
which will quench my thirst for ever.

And since you wait for me at my heart's edge
as did earlier the Samaritan woman at Jacob's well,
    may I plunge often,
    very often,
    into my deepest self,
    and rejoin the *source*
    and drink of this *source*,
    which will never dry up.

My thirst will be quenched then, Lord,
I shall be renewed,
    my troubled waters purified,
    and my words and gestures refreshed.
And I shall be able to return to my brothers and sisters,
    and drink with them the cup of friendship.
I shall not go *unwillingly*
    fearing to waste time,
    but *gladly*

with my heart alive and full of life.
    I too,
      will join in the conversation,
      the laughter
      with expressions and gestures.
And if my friends say on leaving,
    'Many thanks,
      we had a good time together'
I will offer you, Lord, thanks,
    for, owing to you, through me,
they will perhaps have tasted
a few drops of your *living water.*

Jesus said to the Samaritan woman ...   *John 4 v 13*

There was a marriage in Cana of Galilee.   *John 2 vv 1-9*

XVII
LORD, I FEAR FOR MANKIND, FOR IT IS GROWING TOO QUICKLY!

We are proud of the marvellous scientific discoveries and techniques of today's scholars, but we tremble sometimes at their power which grows greater every day. Where are we going? Is proud mankind becoming an apprentice-magician who, in manipulating the universe and life itself, will end by destroying itself?

Nevertheless, it is the wonderful and exciting vocation of mankind to further the creation of the world and of humanity. In the beginning God entrusted humanity with this task. But mankind is not god and "creator" but "co-creator" with Jesus Christ by whom all things were made and without whom nothing was made.

Already for a long time the philosopher Bergson has been calling for "an increase of soul" for our modern world. It equally needs, proportionally, as mankind and its responsibility grows greater, an "increase of love" in Jesus Christ.

Once more, Lord,
turning on my radio,
I learn that mankind has brought about,
    for the first time,
one of those marvels which yesterday
    no-one could have imagined
    that one day he could achieve.
And I don't know any more, Lord,
whether I should admire man's power,
    or should tremble before him,
    sometimes even condemn.

For people have discovered and mastered
the prodigious energy concealed in matter.
They launch hundreds of satellites into space,

77

explore the planets
and prepare to inhabit them.
They invent and make instruments
which can calculate
and work out in a few minutes
what a 1000 human brains
could not do in a thousand hours.
They graft new limbs
on to worn-out bodies.
They make babies in test tubes,
and soon they will be able
to model their faces to taste.
They keep a life in reserve
and hatch it
when they decide to
and as they want to.
They make ... and again they make ...
and they will do it yet again ...
And stupefied, we will discover
that man has come to do
what we thought
God alone could do,
that only yesterday we were begging him for
in useless prayers.

Is man so great,
my God, and his power so great,
that henceforth he will take your place,
relegating you to heaven ...
a heaven which recedes further every day?
Is man a god,
who didn't know it till now,
but who, in growing greater,
is at last discovering his true identity?

Some people think so and say so
    and I cannot believe it.
    I fear for man
    because he is growing too fast!
And yet I believe...

I believe that no scientist in the world
    will ever,
    whatever his machines,
    his calculations,
    and the calculations of his machines,
will ever discover whence comes the *train of life,*   *1*
    where it is going,
    who are the travellers embarked upon it,
    and for what mysterious journey.

I also believe, that the greatest scientists,
    like all of us,
    Lord,
seek someone who loves them
    and whom they can love.
For without bread,
    without water,
    they will perhaps one day be able to make us live
    much better and longer,
but they will never be able to make
a person flourish without love
    ... and more love,
never begin to be able.

I believe, after all, that the greatest scientists,
    like all of us,
    weep when their child dies,
    even if this death is long warded off by them.
And I also believe that in the night they too seek

to know if something of that child,
   some part is still alive.
... But none of their colleagues will ever tell them,
   for they do not know,
   and their science will never tell them.

O Lord, what shall we do tomorrow?
   Is man so proudly distancing himself from you
   and ... losing sight of you?
   If more and more people
   end up believing you are useless ...
   and yet others that you don't exist?
Who will teach us the truth about ourselves
   if it isn't you,
   who said:
I am the Truth ...
   the Light of the World ...
   whoever follows me
   shall not walk in darkness?   *2*
   Who will be able to receive the truth
   since you have said
   that it will never be
conquered by science and scientists
   but only accessible,
to those who are poor in spirit?   *3*

How will man who has become so great
then be able to bring himself to kneel
   to receive this Truth
   in the darkness of faith?

Yes, Lord, I am afraid for man
   for he is growing too fast.
My child, says the Lord,
science is not bad.
You must not be afraid to seek

and discover the secrets of matter,
of life itself.
It is the glory of God to see you grow.
It is man's duty to do everything,
    to raise yourselves up.
But never forget that your spirit,
even so amazingly developed,
    will always remain limited.
Only your heart can be open to the infinite,
    opening itself to my life,
And only my life can allow you to become
    not *like gods*
    but true *children of God.*   4

Do not fear any more man's *power*
    which is developing so amazingly.
The Father of heaven
    is not jealous of his Son's greatness,
    for in creating men creators
    he is sharing his power
    with them as he has wanted to
    since eternity.

It is not their power,
    you should fear,
but what they do and will do with their ever-growing power.
    For, if their spirit
    is enriched with knowledge
    without their heart also
    enriching itself with my love,

then they will build anew towers of Babel   5
    to reach the sky.
    These will sink into the ground,

and they will kill each other.
My child, is it that you fear suffering,
    fruit of man's pride,
    for you and your brothers and sisters?
I understand you.
    I myself was a victim
    but endured that suffering.
Do not doubt the final victory.
for I have overcome the World.

1/ 'In the Paris train, in Life's train'
2/ John 1 vv 8-12
3/ Matthew 11 v 25
4/ Genes.is 3 vv 3-5
5/ Genesis 11 vv 4-8

Some indeed preach Christ of contention, not sincerely …
Philippians 1 vv 15-17

The whole creation waits earnestly for the revelation of the sons of God …
Romans 8 vv 19-22

XVIII
LORD, I AM FAR FROM GIVING YOU THE PLACE WHICH SHOULD BE YOURS.

We think very sincerely that, if people want to build the world and develop humanity without God, they risk catastrophe. But we ourselves – what place do we make for him in our lives? Is Jesus Christ the one who gives sense to our existence? Can we say that the Gospel faithfully illumines our daily paths? And isn't the time that we offer to the Lord often time that's left over – if there is any – when we have fulfilled all our obligations? And those of us who bring up children; what priority do we choose for their lives? Wouldn't it be good to examine our life before Christ from time to time, to hear him say to us, 'What will a man gain by winning the whole world, at the cost of his true self?'

Matthew 16 26

I have said to you, Lord:
    I fear that people,
becoming all powerful through science,
    will end by forgetting you
and will gradually destroy themselves
as they set you aside.   1
    But today I am thinking that,
    in fact,
    I am far, Lord, from giving you the place
    which should belong to you.

I take the time to educate myself,
    inform and cultivate myself
    for I sometimes regret
    not *knowing* more.
I read books,
    some serious ones ...

and others much less so.
I run through newspapers and reviews,
I listen to the radio,
look at television ...

I have good reasons for doing so.
One must be *in the swim*
  and perform well in this demanding world !
  It is necessary, in order to *live well*
  and enable one's family to live well!
  And I find the time,
  I take a lot of time
from the time I have to live.

But time for you, Lord?
  To be *in the swim for you*
  to be informed about you
  to *live better* with you?
You, Lord, come into it ... afterwards
... when I have some spare time.

And, Lord, my children ...?
I want them to succeed in their lives,
  but with what sort of success?
First of all that they learn
  as much as I,
  or more than I.
  I expect it of them,
  push them ...
  and sometimes punish them.
I give them short term goals:
  "this year you go into a higher class,
  this year you have to concentrate on your exams.
  I am not against your activities with young people

your weekend activities ...
but after that ... "
So it is, Lord, that I live in the material world
and act in this way with my children.
And I am appalled at the hypocritical gap
between what I think,
what I say,
and how I *live*.

O, Lord,
Who came among us
to reveal to us the secret of life
and the Way of Love which leads to happiness,
fill us with the desire to meet you,
to know you better
and the hunger to know you more,
in order to follow and serve you better.
Make us *seekers* after God,
not only with the mind
but also with the heart.
Help us to *find time for you,*
not only time snatched
from the futilities which occupy us,
but fresh time,
new time,
as a lover suddenly discovers it
for a love which abruptly erupts
into his well-filled life.

Lord, give to us parents,
who gave life to our children
without them asking for it,
the paramount ambition to make them understand
that this life isn't a gift

to use up for their pleasure alone,
  but a treasure to develop
  so that they may be given pleasure.
Help us to pass on to them the taste for study,
not in order that they should succeed
in acquiring more power
  and ... more money,
but because they are responsible before God
for the gifts they have received,
  and that they must develop them
  for tomorrow,
  to serve you better.

Give us enough true faith
  for them to discover
  that religion is not a lesson
  to learn and know by heart,
  a rule to follow
  to make life more comfortable.
But *Someone* to encounter,
  to know
  and to love.

Help us Lord, I pray you,
  for if by mischance,
  we give them false ideals,
  we will send them on ways that go nowhere.
They will perhaps arrive at acquiring
a few deceptive pleasures,
but they will never find the true happiness
for which they are made.

Help us, Lord,
  for you said to us

'What use is it if you gain the whole world
and lose your life?'   1
And what use is it to help our children
to conquer the world
if they lose theirs?

                                                        1/ Matthew 16 26

He told them a parable "there was a rich man whose land
yielded heavy crops ..."   *Luke 12 vv 16-21*

You are the salt of the earth ...   *Matthew 5 13*

XIX

YESTERDAY EVENING, LORD, I DIDN'T TURN OFF THE TAP IN MY KITCHEN PROPERLY.

A life in the full glare of publicity lit up with sensational activity is not necessarily a full life. Therese, the Child of Jesus, among others, has shown us that on the contrary a life in the shadows, made up of minute little things, can lead to sanctity and shine out to the ends of the earth. The Church has declared the 'little' Therese, the patron of missions.

We often need to make great efforts not to dream of amazing deeds, while forgetting to do conscientiously what we have to do. Dreaming one's life is not living it.

It is God who gives our existence its dimension of the infinite, if we are responsive to him.

Lord, yesterday evening,
I didn't turn off the tap properly in my kitchen.
What does a little drop of water matter,
little,
so little,
falling regularly into the basin?
What can one do with a little drop of water?

But this morning, I found the basin full,
it had overflowed all night.

As you know, Lord, I often despair
at the thousand repetitive acts of my every day life.
So many little things to do,
in the house,
at work,
in all my *ploys*,
little things which seem insignificant to me,
useless,

88

compared with *all there is to do*
compared with what *great people* do,
    the ones one reads about in the newspapers
    and who appear on television
    because they do *great things.*

Since through my circumstances, Lord,
    you invite me
    to be where I am,
    help me to be faithful,
    to live without sensational deeds,
like your mother Mary, who didn't do great things,
but every day
did the little ones very well.
And I will fill my life
with thousands of minute drops of water,
    but well filled.
My life will be productive
because it will flow even at night –
    in the darkness of my days
    as in the darkness of my nights –
it will overflow,
from my heart which doesn't want to withhold it.
And the parched lands
around me will flourish again,
and my neighbours who are thirsty,
will drink from my cup.

For the drops of water of my life
    will, through you, Lord
    have become a river of *living water.*

Jesus said "This is the Kingdom of God: it is like a man throwing seed on the ground".   *Mark 4 vv 26-29*

A woman of Samaria came to the well for water.   *John 4 vv 7-13*

XX
Lord, for a long time I looked at people's faces.

Man is body and spirit, in one. We believe that God has made us "in his own image". So it is 'the whole man', body and 'soul', that is the reflection of God, and in him especially his face, mysterious window of his most profound being..

God spoke in the Old Testament but no person has "seen" him at any time. (John 4 v 12). However, one day God assumed a face, a face like ours, made of the same stuff. Moreover we can say, in a way, that, if God has made us "in his own image and likeness", he made himself, in his son Jesus Christ "in the image and likeness of men".

Yet further. Through his love Jesus Christ has incorporated all men in himself. We have become, as St Paul says, "members of his body". He has given us his Life in our life, and our life, let us not forget, is our spirit and our body united. We are Jesus' brothers, of the same family. It isn't surprising that we resemble each other. Not by the particular features of our faces. Jesus was of the Jewish race, but by 'the family look', that mysterious light that makes real beauty. We must develop that resemblance in ourselves, in our brothers, by welcoming more and more, through Jesus, the Life of God our Father. Then we will pass from having an anonymous – sometimes even disfigured – face, to a transfigured one, and then one day to a face of one resurrected..

From now on in this world, Jesus Christ has no face other than our own and that of our brothers and sisters.

Lord, for a long time I have looked
at people's faces.
> and in their faces at their eyes,
> and in their eyes their expression,
language that is more profound than words and gestures.
I return to you dazzled and overwhelmed,

but always more avid for you.
Faces,
open books from which I have learnt so much,
received so much from my brothers and sisters,
my food,
my communion,
unique faces, special creations,
that no make-up,
no faults,
no wounds
have disfigured permanently
in the eyes of those who know how to look.
What mysterious substance are you made of,
that inscribed in your wrinkles
are the winds and storms,
the rain or sun, open-air lives
as well as secret ones?

Lord, I have admired
the architecture of faces,
cathedrals,
chapels,
or discreet oratories,
And through it I have known the riches
and the poverty of the artist
who fashioned them from within
from each of his or her
thoughts and deeds.

I have suffered cruelly before faces that are wrecked, disfigured,
a reflection of the depths of hidden wounds,
of evil such as
sudden mugging causes.
Then I have seen those lost faces,
adrift
drowned in rain and storm,

While in others, alas, I have only seen
    a few tears escaping
    from submerged torrents.
I have drunk in big gulps
    the light of faces which dwelt in the sun
    and was refreshed by them.
But I have long waited,
as one waits for sunrise,
for a smile to be born on faces of darkness.
I have travelled along the wrinkles
    on ancient faces,
    paths,
    avenues or crevasses,
to discover the traces
    both of joys and griefs
    which have furrowed the clay of long-lived human faces.
    And I return to you,
    dazzled and overwhelmed,
    but always more avid.

    Why, Lord…
    Why am I so fascinated?
And why have I so often undertaken
    these long pilgrimages
    to the sanctuary of faces?

I set off, I own, Lord,
    impelled by curiosity.
Books tell us so little of the mysteries of life,
    that one must search further
    for the light one is looking for.
I had a presentiment of treasure
buried in the dough from which we're kneaded,
    dust,
    living earth,
    inhabited.

Earth mixed with spirit
to the point where one no longer knows,
where is the earth,
where the spirit
in these bodies, these faces,
they are so blended one with another.

I have been seeking *life*, Lord,
beyond the harmony,
of forms and colours.
I have sought the *person*
beyond the personalities.
and beyond the persons I was looking for
…O unimaginable mystery!
    I was seeking
    and suddenly I found
that my hunger for faces, was a hunger for God.
    I was seeking you, Lord,
and you made me a sign.

    O Lord, is it possible?
that some believers
    who sincerely wanted to meet you,
often still wander astray,
    with their eyes on the clouds,
    when they could have perceived you every day
as they passed by their brothers and sisters on the world's ways.
    For since you came to us,
    God, fashioned from the same clay as us,
God who made his face known in Jesus our brother,
    no-one can encounter a person,
    without discovering in him or her something of you.
You, the child of Bethlehem,
    in the faces of babies smiling
    or crying.
You, the runaway of the Temple,
    in the faces of adolescents,

who are not sure
if they are adults or children.
You, tempted in the desert,
in the faces of tormented people,
divided,
torn apart,
by the evil which continually beckons.
You, transfigured,
in the faces of people at prayer,
You, condemned, disfigured,
in the faces of the tortured,
groaning at the blows,
blows to the body,
blows to the heart.
You, the risen one,
in the faces of those whom Love has finally
taken over
and shines, singing out the Easter Alleluia.

Lord, I would like
to continue faithfully,
this uncompleted pilgrimage,
into the faces of my fellow beings.
till the joyful day
when with everyone at last in your Light, contemplating them,
I shall contemplate you.
But still I must
travel long and hard with you
and know you better,
so as to recognise you
in the faces of my fellows.
O Lord, give me
the grace to respect faces.
Never to stare them out of countenance,
trying to grab for myself

the beauties they hold,
or to gather from their lives
the fruits which are ripening for others.
Grant that I may never shut my eyes
　　　to faces of other colours,
to faces which are obscure or repellent to me.
And never to despair in my heart,
even less condemn,
　　　when pride,
　　　　egoism or hatred,
have made faces
into grimacing masks for carnivals of death.

Grant me, on the contrary Lord, the courage
　　　never to stop on the shores of faces,
　　　on attractive shores,
　　　or sad vague bits of ground,
but traveller from afar,
breaking through the visible frontiers,
　　　grant that I may discover
　　　the clear source of Life,
　　　there where in the peaceful lake of the heart
　　　your image slowly emerges.

O grant above all, Lord,
that I may look at faces
　　　a little as you
　　　once looked at them,
　　　when your evangelist said of you
He looked at him and loved him.
Grant me, Lord,
　　　a little of your infinite tenderness,
only a little, I beg you.
And my gaze at the faces

will be warm and caressing.
>Grant me, Lord,
>a little of your purity,
And my gaze at the faces
will be like a sapphire imprinting wax,
and I will release songs long buried,
and I will make cries heard that have been held back too long,
>and tears will flow,
>smiles will beam,
>and, as for me,
>I will hear singing or weeping in those faces,
>and ineffable mystery,
>I will hear you, Lord
>inviting me to sing or to weep
>with them,
>with you, Lord.

God said let us make man in our image"   *Genesis 1 vv 26-27*

He (Jesus Christ) is the image of God invisible.

>*Colossians 1 vv 15-16*

The eye is the light of the body.   *Matthew 6 vv 22-23*

...Master, what shall I do to inherit eternal life.

>*Mark 10 vv 17 & 21*

XXI
LORD, MAKE ME LAUGH!

Many of the faithful think it isn't respectful to laugh in church. On the other hand crying isn't frowned on, rather well regarded. Why one, not the other? It is not a question of confusing noisy distractions and nervous laughter, which are often no more than vain attempts to escape from oneself, from others and from the austerity of everyday life, with healthy pleasure expressed in hearty bursts of laughter.

Should not the joy of being Christian be expressed sometimes. So often we turn serious, preoccupied faces to our fellows. The young say our Eucharists are sad. They are often bored with them. They are not wrong!

It's not easy to be joyful all the time. Is it possible on earth? But it is not impossible to experience in one's heart some moments of real happiness and to share them with our fellows.

To hear real laughter which bursts and crackles like fireworks on the night of 14th July one must go . . . to a convent of nuns at their recreation hour. And look at their faces. And listen.

Why?

Yes, it is Jesus Christ, when he is fully accepted at last into a pure heart, who gives us . . . the wish to laugh.

I don't know why, Lord,
>   when I was praying this morning,
I suddenly realised
>   that I have never imagined you
>   laughing.
laughing a truly hearty laugh, sharing
>   its successive waves,
with others who welcome
>   the richness of this offered joy.
I imagine you as calm, Lord,

sometimes smiling discreetly,
    but above all serious and grave
    and sometimes weeping.
And you know, Lord, that I am happy to know
    that you know how to weep!
But you evangelists didn't think fit to tell us
    that one day on such or such occasion,
    you laughed openly.
And I for one regret it.

I also see you, Lord, as beautiful, luminous,
    transfigured by prayer,
or else with your eyes shining in anger,
flogging the moral hypocrites
    and the religious ones.
I see you disfigured,
    trembling in solitude and fear,
bloody from torture.
But roaring with laughter? ... decidedly not.

Nonetheless you did laugh,   I'm sure of it.
Even if some good souls thnk,
    perhaps,
that it isn't suitable!
    You laughed as a child in Nazareth
when you played in the square with your mates.
    You laughed as an adolescent with your cousins,
in the caravan, returning from the Temple.
    You laughed with your disciples,
    at the wedding at Cana in Galilee,
and you sang,
and you danced if the others danced.
    But afterwards ...
    I find it difficult to imagine! ...

I have pondered why.
I thought it was because ...
I *lack faith!*

I believe that you are God,
without too much difficulty.
Your Father breathed this in my ear,
I am sure of it,
    since you told us that alone
    one could not believe it.
And I thank you for this marvellous gift
    which transforms my life.
    But I admit
    that it isn't easy for me
to believe that you are man.
Not a superman, a man.
A real one.
And that you didn't play at being a man,
    disguised as a man,
    in order to appear to be with us,
    sranding by us for our whole life.

    And nonetheless, Lord,
if I have trouble believing it,
when I meditate on this mystery in my head alone,
it is for me the most marvellous news
which overwhelms me with thankfulness and joy,
    when in my heart I contemplate it.
    For it is in my eyes
    the most sure proof,
    and the most astonishing,
    that from afar you love us all,
    and that this love is near,
    so near that it *touches* us,
    that it takes root in us,

in this humanity that you created,
    but so far,
    so far away from you,
if you had not come.
For you could have loved us from above, Lord,
    and sent an ambassador
    other than you.
    But you *personally* came yourself.
You could have come to be *near us,*
you, God, to lead us.
    and we, men and women, to follow you.
    But you came to us,
    man with us,
    man like us,
    so much like us,
    that we became brothers and sisters.
Brothers and sisters of the baby that cried
    and drank his mother's milk.
Brothers and sisters of the little child who learnt to read,
    and to pray,
Brothers and sisters of the man who preached so well ...
    too well,
    so that he died under torture
    giving his life for us.
    Brother.
    Our brother Jesus,
    who knew how to weep ... and to *laugh* ...
    since he was a man.

I have funny ideas, Lord,
but what can you expect?
To think of you so near to us ...
    so like us
    that we may become like you,
makes me happy,
so happy

that I am astonished that we are not more like you.
And I suffer to see us too serious
    when we talk about you.
And I do not understand why we seem so sad
    when we gather together to pray to you,
    and to offer to the Father, with you,
    your suffering … and your tears,
    your joys … and your laughter,
    your life!
People around us,
    would perhaps believe in you more,
    if we were above all joyful ,
    and if we were seen to be joyful.

Forgive me my frivolity
but this evening I want to say to you
    like little children
    on their big brother's knee
    "Make me laugh!"
Yes, that's my surprising prayer
Lord, make me laugh!
    so that I in my turn
    can make my fellows laugh,
    They need it so much!

That which was in the beginning … that our joy may be complete.
John 1 vv 1-4

Make a joyful noise.
Psalm v 100

XXII
IS IT REALLY FOR YOU, LORD?

*It isn't "for pleasure" that we are involved in such or such movement or service
in the Church or the world. On the contrary, we are sometimes very tired of
all those meetings and activities which "eat up" our time and even earn us
complaints, above all from those we love. But we must seriously question the
authenticity of our actions Much self-interest, pride is often part of it!*
*As Christians, we must be even more vigilant about the presence of Jesus
Christ at the heart of our actions. It is with him that we work.*
*It is difficult for us to live this "gaze of faith" both in our meetings and to
share it in the work place. Nonetheless without "him" we can do nothing.*

Is it really for you, Lord,
 that I went out this evening,
 to attend that meeting?
 It was dark,
 it was cold,
the house was cosy, and my wife engaging.
She let me go without a word,
 only a faint smile with a little kiss,
 but in her expression
 I read
 a sad weariness,
in which I perceived a persistent reproach
 yet again!

She will be asleep when I return
and I will be quiet so as not to awake her,
 while rather wishing
that when I slide into bed
she will turn towards me,

and murmur, half asleep:
"*Were you pleased with your meeting?*"
    Then I will go to sleep a little reassured,
    because I believe
    I am understood a little and forgiven a little.

But is it really for you, Lord,
that I went out this evening?

I drive the car fast,
    I'm late and my friends are waiting for me.
The town around me is already silent, asleep,
    and I realise that I rather admire myself,
    at the thought that I am keeping vigil,
    constant
    in the service of my brothers and sisters.
    However, I drive with my doubts,
    worried,
uneasy with myself and before you, Lord.

Is it really for you that I went out this evening?
Isn't it from habit?
    It's the day for it!
Isn't it to be sure of success for my proposal,
or the motion that I've prepared?...
    We are so few!
Isn't it from pride?...
    Without me they won't be able to...!
Isn't it to defend and push through my ideas?...
    I think them the only right ones!
Isn't it to show my dependability?...
    I will never fail!
Isn't it to make myself feel good?...
    clergy tell us
    to be involved!
Is it really for you?

Sometimes I have fears
    about the value of what I do,
    my intentions,
    my generosity,
    my faith,
    and of running around,
    being busy,
    wearing myself out
    for myself,
    forgetting you.

I drive along with my doubts, Lord
    and gradually
    as you invite me to think of you,
    they dance the more
    their ironic sarabands,
arousing in me a strong longing for recollection,
for finding you in silent devotion...
But I drive on towards noise,
    the tumult of words
    and the excitement of action,
    ...and I know that in a few moments,
    once again,
    I shall forget you,
you, whom I want to serve.

Forgive me, Lord,
because if I believe with all my strength
    that you want to need me,
    to need us,
    to build a world of fellowship,
I must not forget that I need you to make it happen
and work alone,
    battle alone,
    fight alone.
as others do too, I fear,
for we don't often think
to invite you to the meeting,

and when finally we say that you are there,
because it is the custom,
we avoid seeking
and asking you your opinion,
for it is easier to be satisfied with our own,
and more difficult to meditate on your Gospel
and pray to your Holy Spirit.
Nevertheless, Lord,
is it not, '*that we build in vain*
if we don't build with you!'

You are there and I talk to you, Lord,
I entrust this meeting to you,
    and soon
I shall dare to talk about you.
This will be *true* and I shall be true,
    because we shall have had a conversation
    and nourished our love.
And when we return
    together
    in the car,
we shall speak again, about the meeting,
about those who were there
    and about our work.

And if on my return, my wife wakes up,
    Lord,
    you will kiss her,
    won't you,
    when I do?

Verily, verily, I say unto you, he that believeth in me.

John 14 vv 12-13

Abide in me and me in you. As the branch cannot bear fruit of itself, except it abide in the vine.   *John 15 vv 4-5*

XXIII
I am getting old, Lord.

For many old age is a terrible trial. Even if life is often difficult, at the moment that it is ebbing, there are many who try to hang on to it. The greatest suffering is to believe oneself to be condemned to be useless, giving trouble to others, when one would still want to serve It is a time of humility and of purified faith.

But age is not the road to death, but the way to life. Life fully enlightened at last and made divine in Christ for ever. But one must accept the tough transformation, the passage to that other life, as the buried grain of corn must die in order to bring about the new growth.

For the old person the time is past for rushing at others, but not that for "dwelling in Christ as he dwells in us".

John 15 4

That is the condition in which the fruit can ripen.

I am getting old, Lord
   and it's hard to get old!

I can't run any more,
   or even walk fast,
I can't carry heavy loads any more,
   or climb upstairs quickly.
My hands are beginning to tremble,
   and my eyes soon get tired
reading a book,
My memory is getting bad and rebelliously hides from me
   dates and names
      that I really still know.

I am getting old, and ties of affection knotted
    in the course of long years past,
    are one by one loosening,
    and sometimes breaking.
So many acquaintances,
so many beloved people
recede and disappear
    into the remote past,
that my first look at the daily paper
    is to look anxiously at the death notices.

Increasingly, every day, Lord,
    I find myself alone,
alone with my memories.
    and past troubles
which remain alive in my heart,
while I often seem robbed
    of many joys.

Lord, understand me!
You who burned up your life
    in thirty-three intense years,
you don't know what it is to grow slowly old,
and to be there,
with a life that slips implacably away
    from this poor body worn out,
an old vehicle with creaking machinery,
    refusing to work.
And, above all, I have to be there,
    waiting.
Waiting for the time to pass,
time which on some days passes so slowly
    that it seems to mock me,
twisting and turning

in front and around me,
not wanting to yield to the coming night
and to allow me at last … to sleep.
Lord, how is one to believe that today's time,
is the same as in earlier days,
time that went so fast on some days
    in some months,
so fast that I couldn't catch up,
    and it escaped me
before I could live it to the full?

Today I have time, Lord,
too much time,
time that piles up on all sides,
unused.
And I am there, immobilised,
    and good for nothing.

I am getting old, Lord,
    and it's hard to get old,
so hard that I know that some of my friends
    often ask you that this life may end
    because they think their life is
henceforward useless.
They are wrong my child, says the Lord,
and you are too
    not actually saying so,
    but sometimes agreeing with them.
You are necessary
    to all your fellow beings.
And as for me I need you today
    as I needed you yesterday.
For a heart which beats, however worn it is,
    still gives life

to the body it inhabits,
and the love in that heart can flow out,
often more powerfully and purely,
when the tired body at last allows it its place.
Some packed lives,
you know,
can be empty of love,
while others,
which seem very ordinary,
have an infinite warmth.

Look at my mother Mary,
weeping,
unmoving at the foot of my cross.
She was there.
Standing there, certainly,
but she was also powerless,
tragically powerless.

She could do nothing
except be there.
Entirely recollected,
entirely accepting,
and entirely offering herself,
and so with me,
she has saved the world, by giving back to it
all the love lost by mankind,
in the course of time.

With her today,
at the foot of the world's crosses,
all the immense sufferings of humanity are gathered,
dead wood to burn on love's hearth.
But the striving and joys are also gathered,

For gathered flowers are beautiful,
>   but are good for nothing,
>   if they are not offered as gifts,
>   and so many people think about how to live,
>   but forget to give.
Believe me,
>   your life today
>   can be richer than yesterday,
if you accept that you must keep watch,
>   a still sentry in the approaching evening.
And if you suffer because you have nothing left
>   to offer,
Offer your powerlessness
and I tell you that together,
we shall continue to save the world.

Abide in me and I in you. *John 15 vv 4-5*

Jesus said.. there is no man that hath left house... who shall not receive manifold more... *Luke 18 vv 29-30*

When I speak with tongues of men and angels, and have not charity... *1 Corinthians 13 vv 1-3*

XXIV
I WENT OUT, LORD, BUT MY STOCKING LADDERED.

We are sure of ourselves too often, and when the unforeseen occurs in our lives, from minor incidents to violent storms, we, who thought ourselves standing upright, find ourselves on the ground. We are aware then of our weakness. It is because we rely on our own strength.
Only God can, through our efforts, make us certain of the faithfulness that we have promised him..

I went out, Lord,
  but my stocking laddered.
I was late leaving for work,
  but my shoelace broke.
I was watching the match on television,
  but the telephone rang.
I was hurrying along in the street,
  but I met a friend,
  he talked …
  and talked …
  without giving me time to tell him
  that someone was waiting for me.
At last I got to sleep,
  but the child cried
  because he woke up.

It's the unforeseen, Lord,
  in my well arranged life,
like a ball in a good game of skittles,
there I am in disarray.
I am unnerved,

irritated,
sometimes
I even attack those close around me,
holding them responsible.
And the peace in my heart disappears abruptly.

Trying to follow in your way, Lord,
I make great efforts.
Too sure of myself
I often believe I'm getting there.
But disappointed,
humiliated,
today I perceive
that I accept your way,
only …
when I know the road and the stages of the journey.
Before the unforeseen
I stumble violently
and my good intentions
disappear or are spilt on the ground.
I believed myself faithful
and find myself unfaithful.

My life, Lord,
is not near enough to you.
I am not with you enough.
And nonetheless you are there
in my well organised life,
as in the unforeseen times.
You don't enjoy the difficulties which arise,
but you are always available
if I want you
to help me live each day as it comes.

Give me, Lord, I beseech thee,
the peace which once you promised your disciples,
not my peace,
    hat which in my pride
    I create for myself by effort of will,
    that which in my vanity
    I feel safely surrounded by,
but yours.
Which I receive from you,
which is not affected
    either by wind,
    or by storm.
Then the unforeseen will be for me,
    a test of faith,
    a measure of faith,
    a question of love which awaits
    my loving response.
And through this I will say to you, Lord,
    "You can see that I love you!"

Peter said to Jesus … before the cock crows.   *John 13 vv 37-38*

I leave you my peace …not as the world gives.   *John 14 v 27*

XXV
IT WAS A HUGE AND OLD ROCK, LORD.

How could man, who can only look at himself with simple human sight, not be seized with terrible vertigo when he becomes aware of his smallness before the hundreds of millions of men and women in the past, present and future human race. Who is he? What value is his life, a minute drop of water in an immense ocean, a few moments in millions of years?

In the same way that in a big family each child enjoys the total love of its parents and a new one receives it equally without taking anything away from his brothers and sisters, so the love of 'our Father who art in heaven' reaches us all personally ... everlastingly.

Because we are unique limbs in the great body of humanity we are indispensable, each in our place, and our life is not a life which passes, leaving only a few traces, it is, in Jesus Christ and through him, life eternal.

It was a huge and old rock, Lord,
on a very old path which led to the village,
   high up.
I was told that this path was,
   from the earliest times
the route of passage of a multitude of invaders,
   of travellers and of pilgrims,
and that hundreds
and hundreds of thousands of people
   had trampled on these flagstones
   without effacing them.
And contemplating this hard rock,
   (hollowed out like a quarter moon,
   polished like a pebble),
   a durable impassive witness,
I feel giddy in my smallness.

Who am I, Lord, who pass so quickly
over this which endures?
It has borne the weight of hundreds
and hundreds and hundreds of years,
and I make only one step,
among thousands of other steps,
steps which have vanished,
while it keeps watch, unmoving,
a hard rock which endures, to remind me of my smallness.

What traces have they left, Lord,
all those travellers in time,
the countless mass of people
who have lived before me?
Their combined millions have hardly managed
to change the shape of this hard rock.

Where are they now then, those tiny ant-like people,
who passing high above by the village,
swing one by one out of time
at the end of their life's journey?
Where are they, those millions of 'disappeared'?
I don't see them any more,
I don't hear them any more,
… whereas I see this hard rock which endures
to remind me of my smallness.

Who am I then, Lord,
I who am so small and would like to be so big?
I who reckon my days and years,
and am no more than a moment!
What's the use of living
if my life is nothing but a second in millions of years?
What's the good of fighting

if my efforts and suffering
are nothing but imperceptible sighs
in the immense clamour of innumerable human beings?
What's the good of laughing if my bursts of laughter,
hardly heard, are lost,
a fleeting spark in the terrifying night of time?

What's my life worth then, Lord?
the worth of each step,
each word, each gesture,
my tears and smiles,
I who want them to be great and important
to the point of dreaming them
into the dimension of eternity?

But above all, Lord, above all,
how to believe, that I, who am so small
should be so big in your eyes?
How could you want me and wait for me
one among the millions of people of the future?
How can you notice me today,
a minute grain of sand on the world's beaches,
a drop of water in the vast rivers
which flow and disappear into the ocean?
How can you love me
among all the others you have to love,
and how will you be able to remember me
when the tiny flame of my life is snuffed out,
and, as I want to believe,
it goes to rejoin the millions of flames
which still burn before you
and will burn to eternity?
O tell me, Lord,
In front of this hard rock which endures,

which disturbs me and sets me at naught,
I need to hear you say again that you love me,
    as you have told me that you do love me ...
    in spite of my smallness.

Yes, I love you my child, says the Lord,
and your life is precious to me
    for it doesn't *exist alone,*
and your life came directly from my Father's heart.
    But you see, life
    isn't like the footsteps of people,
    separated one from another,
it is a river which flows in each of you,
    millions though you be.
You receive it from others and you must pass it on
    and others receive it from you,
    to give it again.
That is what life is, my child: life that is given.
    If you keep it for yourself you die,
    if you pass it on you live
... and your footsteps, words, actions and smiles
will live in your brothers till the end of the world.

But listen further,
your life is so precious to me
that I offer you my own,
    if you accept and receive it into yours,
    then your footsteps, your words,
    your actions and your smiles will overcome death
and, breaking through the doors of time,
    will burst forth into my eternity.
Go in peace. I tell you again that I love you
    and that my Father loves you, personally,
like millions of your brothers and sisters,

for real love never diminishes
    when it is shared among everyone,
and your Father is God,
and his love is infinite.
Thank you, Lord, O thank you for your love,
and thank you, hard enduring rock,
    if I could I would take you away,
    would make you a stone altar.

The Kingdom of God is like a mustard seed ...

Matthew 13 vv 31-32

For as we have many members in one body ...

Romans 12 vv 4-6

XXVI
Prayer with the night workers.

*A huge crowd of people gets up to go to work in the night; the majority of
them have not chosen this ordeal but are compelled by necessity.*
*Some men and some women get up in the night to go and pray in the chapel
of their abbey. They have chosen to keep vigil before God on behalf of their
brothers and sisters.*
*The first, the great majority, don't think of offering their labours to the Lord
but the second welcome them and carry them to present to him. Thanks to
them, one must believe, God hears this dramatic chorus of human endeavour
which every night rises to him from the earth.*

It is late, Lord,
and I would like to sleep.
    I need to sleep.
But this evening I think of the night workers,
of that multitude of people who work
    while we sleep,
    manufacturing what we need
    to live on.

I have often seen
    workers' transports
    collecting them from around the town
    and from the more remote countryside,
    their manual skills subjugated
    to the demands of the factory.
They work like remorseless metronomes for ballets without intervals,
beating out the rhythm of the life of an army of workers.
I have met people

whose bodies and exhausted nerves
couldn't stand the rhythm.
They lead broken lives
which nothing and nobody can repair.
I have known shattered couples
in which the husband and wife
only communicate
through words scribbled
on the kitchen table.
I have played quietly with children
who are condemned to daytime silence
... because daddy is sleeping.

I don't understand, Lord.
You invented night,
isn't it for sleeping?
When your sun first gently goes down,
extinguishing its light, it invites repose.
But people have thought up night work
and day-time sleep.
They turn on neon lighting,
then shut the shutters
to make believe night is day and day is night.

They say that in order to respond
to the demands of the modern world,
nature must be adjusted *at any price.*
They say that the economy rules,
that it commands and must be obeyed
and that the machinery must be serviced,
by day and by night.
Finally they say that here or there

they are studying new *conditions of work,*
    trying to rehumanise
    what has been dehumanised.
But you know why, Lord…
    that output maybe better
    and yield higher!
Man remains a slave
    and suffering goes on,
    that vast suffering
    and those cries
    and that wailing are so quickly stifled,
And man is conditioned to the point where he no linger thinks
    of when he will go to sleep
    because it has always been like this!
    and it has to be!

But this evening I can hear, Lord,
    this immense clamour,
and before closing my eyes
    and giving myself up to you,
I want to offer you,
    not those undeserved sufferings –
    you condemn them –
    but this burden of labours
    inflicted on people
    and this marvellous generosity
    that they proclaim every day.
For why do these night workers rise
    if not to earn bread for their wives
    and for their children?
And even if some of them
    are driven by the attraction of pleasures
    which the rich so easily pronounce unnecessary,

where other people are concerned.
it is an amazing love song
which is raised every night
    ... while we are sleeping.
But Lord, does it reach you?
    So many people, alas,
    don't know for whom their lives are singing
    beyond,
    well beyond
    their earthly loves.
Bend your ear, Lord,
listen I beseech you,
so that so much effort isn't lost,
    so much pain
    and so much love lived through.

Forgive me, Lord,
why doubt you
and not believe that this night-time hymn
    perhaps
    rises higher towards you
    than our facile chanting
    in cosy gatherings,
since they mean more than our pleasant words?
They are words of life
    marked with the blood of toil.

Forgive me, Lord,
    why should I doubt you
    and why doubt them?
When mingled with this nocturnal choir
some very pure voices are raised,
    those of the men and women,
    who rise before dawn,

watchers of the night,
    those voluntarily
    singing your praises,
    hidden in an abbey,
soloists of pure love,
    ambassadors of humanity,
    who accompany the shut mouths
    and perhaps even the shut hearts
    of the crowd of night workers.

I believe Lord,
I believe
... but tell me this evening
    that you hear them *all*.

Yes, my child, says the Lord, I hear;
    for all men and women are my brothers and sisters,
    even if they don't know it,
    and no song of love rises from the earth
    without reaching me.
And I welcome them all,
    even the false notes,
    and I pass them on to the Father
    in infinite praises.

There are diversities of spiritual gifts.   *1 Corinthians 12 vv 4-7*

Jesus sat before the treasury and saw how the people cast money into the treasury.   *Mark 12 vv 41-44*

Straightway Jesus constrained his disciples to get into a ship... he went up into a mountain to pray.   *Matthew 14 vv 22-23*

XXVII
LORD, WE INVITE YOU INTO OUR NEW HOUSE.

Many people, and especially couples, dream of owning a house of their own one day, a home where one can be oneself, take root and bring up a family. But this ambition often conceals many snares. The house for which one has longed for so long can become an engrossing preoccupation; it has to be paid for, equipped. Sometimes it takes up a lot of time and energy so that the owners neglect other necessary tasks. In the end it can become a prison for those who shut themselves inside it. To be rich in one way or another is not bad – if it's a matter of obviously deserved well-being – but it is a responsibility. To own a house is a legitimate luxury if it allows one to bring up one's family and to serve other people better.

W̲e dreamt of a house, Lord,
    I dreamt of a house,
    and the house is there,
    ours.

Placed above freshly turned–over ground
    it grew rapidly.
Every evening it awaits me, faithful,
and like open arms the big shutters
    signal and call to me from afar.
    It's our home.
    It's my home.
Our house, Lord,
new, beautiful.

Now we have to pay for it,
    we will have to make sacrifices.
Now we must furnish it,

we will devote ourselves to this.
Now we must live in it,
    ... and that is not so simple,
for the walls of our house conceal traps,
Lord,
    the enemy has put them there.
    as sometimes in embassies,
and thinking it over,
    we detected some this evening,
    some cleverly camouflaged,
    some avoiding our hearts' radar,
while some others, alas, are so alluring
that we have already allowed ourselves to be caught.

Understand us, Lord,
you who have suffered certainly,
from having "no place to lay your head",
we too have suffered,
    from that cramped flat,
    where it was always noisy,
    together with those dirty stairs
which by the evening we could hardly bear to climb,
    from those grey walls around us,
    behind us,
    which hid the sky from us
    and from those neighbours,
    forgive us Lord ...
    who were so hard to bear.

Understand us.
We waited so long,
we dreamed for so long,
... and waited because we dreamed,
that today we have a great wish

to go home,
to rest,
to curl up in this warm interior,
as in a mother's womb,
sometimes to light the wood fire
which merrily sings and dances.
in front of the dull radiators
which heat without smiling,
to look at the flowers in the garden
planted in open ground,
in real earth, Lord,
earth which has escaped from the cement sheath
and from black tar.
We have a great wish to stay at home,
on our own,
not to go out at all some evenings,
not to join in this or that party,
sometimes not even to reply to invitations
from people expecting us
at their homes,
and only to open *our* door
to very close friends
who will come to add a few flowers,
to the bouquets of our delights.

And nonetheless, Lord,
as you know,
our dreams of a house were often generous dreams.
We wanted a dwelling where we could rest
but rest in order to serve more.
We wanted an open house,
where other people,
all other people,
could come and go

as they come and go to their own homes.
A house where one rings the bell,
    enters,
    sits down,
    rests
    and is refreshed,
A house which one goes out of feeling lighter
    because burdens have been shared,
    sometimes even shed.
A house which one finally leaves
    richer, because one has been served with a meal of friendship.

But now, Lord,
    this evening we are worried
because we have found *the traps*
    in the house.
We need you in order not to fall into them
and to be aware of those we do not want to see.
    Stay with us, Lord,
    for it is late,
    and the night is coming,
thick and dark into our tired hearts.
Stay with us and be at home in our home.
With all our heart *we invite you into our new house.*

My children, says the Lord, be happy,
for your house is beautiful
    in its innocent beauty,
    the traps are in your hearts
    and not in its walls.
If your hearts are closed, doors and shutters are closed
    and you are in prison.

If your hearts are open, doors and shutters open too
    and you can go out
    and others come in.
Open your hearts wide
    and I will come to you,
    as I did formerly to Martha and Mary
    and their brother Lazarus,
    and, if you wish it,
    I will share my Word with you
    and you will share bread with me
and I shall be content in your house
    if others are content there.

I will come
more often than you think ...
but I shall come in disguise...
    ... and on some evenings of exhaustion, alas,
will you recognise me
in the importunate one who turns up?

Whosoever cometh to me ... he is like a man who built a house and
digged deep ...   *Luke 6 vv 47-49*

If a man love me ... and I will make my abode with him.
                                     John 14 v 23

XXVIII
He asked for "a lemonade for two".

In today's world the drama which dominates all the other dramas is that of the underdevelopment of a huge section of humanity compared to the development and over-development of the rest.

The permanence of the problem causes us to get used to it, only stirred up now and then by a violent shock to our sensibility. Furthermore we often cease to react to the increasing enormity of it: "What can we do about it?"

The developed countries only think of developing themselves still more. They bury themselves in their problems, seemingly not wanting to understand that they will never be able to resolve them without resolving them together with those of all humanity.

A peaceful world cannot be founded on an immense injustice. The Church itself in its concerns turns in too often on itself. It sinks into internal problems at the expense of its missionary tasks. It does not set an example of sharing. In spite of the appeals of successive Popes the dioceses relatively better endowed with priests have only sent a few of them to the impoverished dioceses of Africa, Latin America and Asia. The Church organises charities, aids "victims" of under-development, sometimes heroically, even helping them ... to die. But it doesn't attack the causes of under-development. It's not its role it says. When some priests risk doing so, they are often called to order, even condemned. Finally, if the Church is prompt to remind us of our moral responsibilities in the domain of sexuality for example - in spite of some official brave publications, little known because of their feeble showing in the media - it is in general less prolix and vehement about our economic and political responsibilities ... in the face of world problems.

The drama of the underdeveloped peoples and its appalling catalogue of suffering and death is the greatest collective sin of our times. For christians it is Jesus Christ who dies each day in the millions of his brothers and sisters. Together we are all responsible.

He asked:
'one lemonade for two, please'
    and the waiter replied:
'that's not possible sir'.
    They looked at each other, he and she,
    he hesitated,
then resignedly ordered two lemonades.

They were thirty or perhaps 35 years old,
they were poor certainly, but in no way tramps.
I watched them, Lord,
    for a long time.
    They did not exchange a single word
    and hardly any glances.
I left, carrying them in my heart.

I bring them to you this evening,
    my unknown friends,
    my brothers in passing.
I know that you saw them
    when I saw them,
    but a brother has the right,
    hasn't he,
To speak to his father about his unlucky brothers and sisters?

I know nothing, Lord,
about these two
    except the visible sign of their hidden sufferings.
But now I recognise the wound
    that they have reopened
    in my tender heart
    without knowing
that the would unleash a storm.

For my heart is a volcano,
prompt to flare up
and brutally vomit
    a thousand flames
    which have been repressed for too long.

You know it, Lord,
I suffer from it
and I often wish that you would give me
    a peaceful heart,
    a docile heart-beat …
    which will let me sleep.
    But I am made like this
and I thank you for it.
So much the worse for my suffering.

But I don't want this fire of mine
    to flare up too often,
to be transformed into petrified lava
    in a desert of death.
Also, Lord, this evening,
receive my anger,
    and my distress,
    and my outbursts,
    and, in my prayer,
    my words
    like flaming arrows.
I have only my revolt to offer
but I am sure that, through your love,
you can transform this untamed force
    into a mysterious energy,
    capable of moving mountains.

'*One lemonade for two*',
these were their words.
But other words,
>   so often read,
>   so often heard
>   and so often buried,
>   forgotten,
recur to me,
and like wild beasts that have escaped from their cages,
>   dance in my head
>   this evening
>   in infernal sarabands ...

One litre of polluted water for one or ten families.
One sack of corn or rice for a whole village.
One school for a whole district.
One hospital for a whole province.
... ...   One priest for 100,000 people.
>   One,
>   *One,*
>   Always one
>   for ten,
>   for a hundred,
>   for a thousand and ten thousand,
while we have ten,
>   a hundred,
>   a thousand ... for one.
And at the end of these figures, there is the bill
>   and the precise accounting,
>   terribly precise.
For many groups of experts
>   calculate,
and they know how to calculate,
>   calculate precisely

with their precise machines.
Everywhere people are sitting down,
    considering,
    discussing,
and writing precise reports based on precise figures.
And millions of people read them
    and say the account is good.
    And this account,
    these figures,
these are people
hundreds of thousands of men and women
who die and who should not die!

These are hundreds of millions of children,
    with bloated bellies
    skin and bone
    surviving for three or four months
    or two or three years ...
while a few small babies
in their perfected incubators
    will live their lives out
    thanks to an army of doctors
    and of devoted nurses.

These are the hundreds of millions of illiterate people
    who will remain *half-witted*
while millions waste their time and fool around
    in universities.

These are the hundreds of millions of disabled people
    and sick people in agony
while an emotionally appealed–to crowd
    generously raises money

for a single heart
which is about to stop beating,
or for a single little child
whose eyes are dimming…
These are the hundreds of millions of people
who would like to know you better,
Lord,
you who said:
"I came so that they should have Life
and have it in abundance",
and about whom I will never be made to believe
that it is solely a question
of the life of *their souls*.
As if your Life could flourish
on a heap of corpses!
As if you had not said to your apostles
"Feed them"
and to the crowd
"Share the bread and the fish"
and to us all:
'I was hungry
and you did not feed me'.
These are the hundreds of millions of people
who would like to know you,
while the bishops
hesitate to send them one or two of their priests
because they no longer have in their diocese
the two or three hundred that they think necessary.
While pious parishioners get up petitions
demanding to retain
their devoted vicar for themselves.
While a body of good christians protest
because they no longer have
their chaplain

present at every meeting.
And all the while, Lord,
while every day,
    surely,
    inexorably,
    millions of people die
    who ought not to die,
or politicians,
because we demand it of them,
struggle with *our* problems,
    real problems,
    but little ones,
    very little ones,
    only touching briefly
    in their wise speeches
    on the main drama
    monstrous
    unbearable
of that part of humanity
    which suffers in agony before our eyes.

And all the while, Lord,
your Church laments
    and makes huge efforts
to retain a few thousand of its members,
    who move away from it
    because they disagree with a decision
    and doubt the Eucharist
    when they change the vestments.
Your Church assures us faithfully,
    that it's - it's a sin to take the pill
    and a very serious sin
    to abort a child who should be born
but *it doesn't declare to us strongly enough*
that it is equally monstrous

to force millions of little boys
and little girls
to prostitute themselves
for a mouthful of bread,
and to allow the lives
of hundreds of millions of children
to be cut short
who are born
and live and die before our eyes.
And all the while, Lord,
I, making such a noisy protest,
am pleased with my holy anger,
proud of it ...!
In my head I revolve beautiful ideas
and remain passive.
I reassure myself with some knowing excuses,
a few generous gestures,
And yet I know,
I know *that the accounts are right*
and that the *figures are people.*

O Lord,
grant me I beseech you,
never to have the indecency to pity myself,
even if I am poor
in comparison to those richer than I,
never to waste –
knowing the shame of those who have possessions –
and to teach my children to waste nothing
showing them the value of bread
and of the butter on the bread.
Grant me the will
to seek material help
for the organisations which battle
for the development of the third world,

for a quarter of the world,
instead of criticising,
    judging,
    from my elevated sufficiency,
and let me be persuaded
that the engagement of the general conscience, by the drama
of that section of humanity which is dying,
    will one day force people
    to organise themselves to relieve it.
Help me never to be silent,
    but to speak out unceasingly,
    to shout,
    even if I upset people,
    even if some want to stifle my shouts,
    even if some people label me a red,
    and even if my friends don't understand me.

There, Lord,
I don't hold it against myself,
    I have warned you.
In my prayer you see the wheat and the tares
    and you will sort it out.

    The volcano has died down
    but I beseech you,
    even if I must suffer,
    do not extinguish the fire!

The rich man and Lazarus.   *Luke 16 vv 19-21*

What use ... faith and not works.   *James 2 vv 14-17*

The harvest is abundant but the workers are few.
                                 St. Matthew 9 vv 36-38

XXIX
I AM NOT AFRAID OF YOU ANY MORE, LORD!

Religion based on fear is finished. Almost finished.

It is true that some of the faithful have dropped 'religious practices' as their fear of not being in order diminishes. If fear is the beginning of wisdom it is never the beginning of love, and religious observances without real faith are more seriously hypocritical. than are loving gestures without love. Wasn't the Lord clear enough about this?

Sin and confession are no longer in fashion. But if the sense of sin has been lost it is not that sin is talked about less, but that for too long it is discussed as a lack of rules and regulations. As for confession, .we have emptied it of meaning. Many priests gave up encouraging it and many of the faithful, gradually realizing the absurdity of it gave it up.

Since the Council, hope has been reborn. Many Christians rediscovered or discovered the marvellous meaning of Reconciliation. They returned. But the rules and regulations also returned!

Please God that the Church doesn't start brandishing hellfire again to bring people back to the faith! But it is human weakness to get what one wants from another by fear, even for his or her good, and lack of faith to believe that love is measured by the merits of the beloved.

The love of God is infinite and free. Preaching this is difficult, but it is the heart of faith. And it is easier to help people to follow a carefully constructed set of rules than actually to live their lives as a response to Jesus Christ our Saviour.

When prohibitions sound louder than love songs they will end one day by killing love.

I am not afraid of you any more Lord!
    I feel light,
    free,
    happy,

and I thank you for it.
Because I admit that I was a bit afraid of you ...
Only a little bit wasn't it?
    But it was too much.
For in my silent heart,
vaguely anxious from time to time, I was thinking
    that following you trembling
    wasn't following you at all.

It wasn't my fault, Lord,
I was told so many things!
and many things which were not said any more
    but which hang on in our memories,
    poisoning our hearts.

I was told that it was bad
    to do this
    because it was a sin,
    and still worse to do that,
    because it was a mortal sin,
and that I should be punished for sin,
    temporarily for small ones,
    and eternally for big ones...
unless I asked forgiveness
in order to avoid the pain.
    For it was enough
    to go to confession,
    and to go every time
    that I committed a mortal sin.
And so it is Lord,
    that as a young child
    I thought...
forgive me,
that to avoid eternal punishment it was enough
not to torment yourself for your whole life

but to repent, to repent well.
For we were then reminded
that we know neither the day nor the hour
        as you yourself told us.
And some sincere and zealous prophets
immediately threatened hell fire
        to bring back to you
        the lost sinners.
The greater the fear,
the greater the number returning
and the greater the joy.
        That was in times past..
        but a past
which has marked today's grandmothers.
And if I talk of them this evening, Lord,
        it is that some of the faithful
        regret this past.
They complain that priests
        only talk about.. love
        and not about sin
        and eternal pain.
If they were more severe, they say,
they would fill the churches, which are emptying
and people would be happier in themselves
        if they were more afraid.

It's horrible, Lord!
I don't judge the hearts I believe to be sincere.
But how can anyone
distort your message to this point?
        For all that was true...!
        But is it *really true*
        to talk to a living person
        only about illness and how to heal it

about death and how to avoid it?
    Is it *really right*
to fossilise love into calculated gestures
    the total of which can be checked
    precisely and minutely
and thus goodness be measured
by all the established norms?

How can one believe, Lord,
    without misrepresenting it
that love can one day be born of fear,
    and if heaven means to love,
    as one knows love in y*ou*
    how can any sort of fear
    one day be the preparation for it?

How can one believe, Lord,
    that to follow you it is enough to keep the law
    and regularly to perform some religious rites,
    without scrupulously checking
    the state of one's heart?
    One's heart which sometimes beats
    regularly,
    along by-roads,
when its no longer keeping to
    straight and beautiful roads.

How can we believe that heaven *has a value*,
    that we have to *win it*
    by putting a price on it
    as if love was for sale
    and not free.

But how difficult it is, Lord,
to believe enough in this love

and to live each day alert enough
to be able *to receive it from you!*
Lord I must ask you to forgive me,
for if I haven't actually trembled with fear before you,
sometimes I have
    like many people,
        thinking about death
        and what happens after death,
        thoughts which are disturbing and mysterious,
tried to act *correctly*
    in order to protect myself.

Nonetheless, Lord,
sometimes perceived you a little more closely
    and you captivated me.
yet I didn't follow you,
you who were beckoning to me. ,
I was satisfied with a *respectable* life
    and with more or les regular observances
thinking it was enough to be *correct*
    in order to be at peace.

But your love is constant, Lord,
    and you accompany us
    and on my daily road
    I have gradually recognised you,
    and slowly discovered you.
    YOU.
    You who came to reveal that God is Love,
    nothing more,
you who taught us to say

Our Father,
    for we are his children,
you who gave us one commandment:
        to love one another.
You who gave the Church into the charge
    of your first representative on earth,
    asked him only:
    "Peter, do you love me?"

It was you, Lord, that I should have followed
and followed out of love.

Lord, I don't regret, .
but on the contrary a thousand times I thank
    the priests who have finally made me understand
    that you have loved us first.
That the heart of faith is first to believe it,
        then *to allow oneself to be loved,*
and that the essential in religion
    is to love you and to love all our brothers and sisters
    as you have loved us.

I am not afraid of you any more, Lord,
and it isn't fear that gets me on my feet
        trying to follow you.
I am not pure, for sure,
        you know it,
        far from it!
But when I pray to you it seems to me
    it is not any longer to maintain
    an important relationship,
which will produce unknown numerous advantages,

but I dare to say. . .

    it is because I love you,

because I want to develop our friendship.

And with you

serve all my brothers and sisters better.

And now I dream. . .

    sometimes,

    I am proud of it,

    and I am mad with joy,

I dream of seeing you face to face,

    of letting myself love you at last,

    of loving you without reserve,

and of one day seeing

all people gathered together as brothers and sisters,

as a family

    around our Father.

The only fear remaining to me,

    and I suffer because of it,

is the fear

of not loving enough

as you do,

gratuitously.

The Lord is my light and my salvation; whom then shall I fear?

Psalm 27 v 1

Stand fast therefore in the liberty wherewith Christ hath made us free.   *Galatians 5 vv 1–13*

Peace I leave with you, my peace I give unto you.   *John 14 v 27*

XXX
Lord, I would like to be sure that you are fighting with me.

Many Christians are committed to the Church. They are needed, more and more. Others are committed to good works. They are equally needed. The injured ask for good Samaritans. But the people committed to unions, politics ... are fewer. They are much despised by many people and some even condemn them ...if they are not of the same opinions as themselves.

Don Helder Camara said with a smile: "When I devote myself to the poor they say I'm a saint. When I denounce the structures which produce the poor, they say I'm a communist".

To care for victims is praiseworthy, but even more so is it to battle against the 'structures of sin' of which Jean-Paul II speaks. They produce victims and menace peace. It is the social dimension of charity.

For sure the worlds of economics, of social science, of politics are tough worlds and their fight is sometimes violent. It frightens Christians. But all violence is not to be condemned. Parents who fight to defend their child who is in danger are "violent" people but it is the violence of love. And the Church has never condemned "defensive" war(!), or people who stand up against oppression, only hate is not of God. May Christians not snipe at their brothers and sisters who "rise up" in just and necessary battles. May they bring love into the fight, with the Lord!

Lord,
I and my comrade are fighting,
    loyal to my *movement,*
      to my *organisation,*
solid in the fight
for a more humane and just life.

But the battle is rough,
and I very often fear
to embark on it without you.

Lord,
I would like to be sure, that you are fighting with me!
People, alas, are needed for defence
when war breaks out.
One day perhaps everyone will lie down
refusing to take part,
but that won't be tomorrow.
and today
there are so many causes to defend
and also wars to fight,
for which combatants are mobilised.
People are needed to look after the wounded
and bury the dead,
for the victims are countless
who are searching earnestly for justice.
People are needed to sign treaties,
when some wars finally come to an end.
But more is needed,
much more
to *avert wars by making peace,*
the peace which can only flourish
in a just world.

I hesitated for a long time
before engaging in this battle for peace.
With the other snipers I soothed my conscience
with the educated maxim
that one person on their own
cannot raise up the world.

I avoided suspect groups
       who make revolutions...
The worlds of economics,
       unions,
       politics,
       were for me polluted worlds.
And I was afraid of sullying my heart if I plunged into them.
But Lord I was not at peace.
Wasn't it you
       who often called out to me
       through events?
For you said one must love one's brothers and sisters,
but loving them
is not just smiling at them,
       first extending them a hand
       then willingly extending the first cheek
       and pardoning them with the second!
If they have nothing to eat,
if they are ignorant, exploited,
       and above all deprived of bread,
       of dignity,
can I send them home,
       with my hand still clasping my hundred francs,
saying to them
       'I love you'
       or at least
       'I will pray for you'?

I am 'committed' but it's hard as you know.
For if one admires and respects
       those who fight
       and give service
       when war is raging,

those who try to create a fraternal world
    in this unjust and cruel world
    are often criticised,
    and sometimes severely condemned.
You have pushed me on,
I beg you not to leave me on my own,
for full of passion
I find myself in the roughest conflicts
attacked …
    blows rain on me
    from my adversaries,
    and sometimes my friends,
ill judged …
    I am classed as too *rightist*
    or too *leftist*
    or *too much in the centre*,
    each giving me a different position.
I search and I search myself.
And sometimes I have doubts.

For the battle is not straightforward
and that's where I suffer.
And the battles are so fierce
    that often I admit
    I lose sight of you.
    Alone,
    in the evening
    before you,
    I regret,
    I am ashamed,
    and I wait for your forgiveness.
For if I want to fight,
I want it to be with you.

Hear my prayer, Lord,
　　for if I know
　　　that our human institutions
　　　are not the Kingdom
I also know that yeast needs dough to make it rise.
　　And dough needs flour.
　　And flour needs corn.
　　And the corn, flour and dough,
demand our handiwork
　　for the bread to be cooked,
　　and that from this bread,
　　you make the Eucharist.

Lord,
grant me I beseech you,
　　the yeast of your love!
Help me not to judge and condemn
　　those who sit quietly in the wings
watching us fighting in the arena,
　　and save me from jealousy
　　seeing them without scruple
　　profiting from our victories
　　forgetting that they owe them to us.

Help me to understand
and to accept
　　that people living the same faith
　　have opinions
　　that are opposed to mine
and enable me to communicate at the same table
　　as those against whom I fight.

Grant that loyalty to my movement,
    my faction,
may never be absolute for me.
I am a rebel of conscience
    and accept what I must do
    and loyally obey,
while I often revolt
when your Church speaks
    and sometimes refuse to follow her directions.
Grant me then
    the strength to say no
when my conscience refuses to say yes.
    And the courage to accept
    the reproaches of friends
    who accuse me of treason,
    because for me it is a matter
  of true faith.

Help me to ponder your Gospel,
not looking for *formulas*
that are not to be found there
    but to be nourished by your word,
so that it will cause
good grain to grow in my ground
and, flourishing, produce good news for my brothers and sisters
and ripen for them
into fruits of justice and peace.

Finally grant me, Lord,
    that supreme grace ...
    that you alone can give
    of loving my adversaries
    as much as my allies,

not only secretly
in my good feelings,
     but by listening to them,
     respecting them,
     trying to understand them,
     and to believe
     that sincerity,
     generosity,
     are not my sole preserve,
but that they can exist in others,
     even if they are enemies.
For you know my passionate nature, Lord,
that perhaps I immerse myself too quickly
in my passion for justice!
     Sometimes I so long for vengeance
     and to hurt in my turn he who wounded me …
     that I find it difficult,
     oh yes, very difficult to forgive.

Grant me, Lord, the strength to forgive.

I am with you, says the Lord,
I am with you in your battles,
for I am with all those who fight
     to defend their brothers and sisters,
     even if they venture into far lands,
     far from a safe enclosure
     where the fearful drowse.
But examine your heart, my child,
     for I cannot be
     where there is hatred,
and only love can assure you of victory
     and assure you of mine.

Why do you doubt, you man of little faith?
    happy are you!
    happy are all of you
    who dare to risk going forth,
    with both hands and feet,
    into the battles for justice.
For I did not come
for those who keep their hands clean
    because they remain sitting
    with their hands in their pockets.
Fear not!
I washed my disciples feet,
    and, if the combatants' feet
are dusty,
    I shall wash theirs too.

What doth it profit ... though a man say he hath faith and have not
works...   *James 2 vv 14-17*

Hereby we perceive the love of God, because he laid down his life for
us ...   *John 3 vv 16-18*

XXXI
All this isn't me!

It so happens that we can be brought to despair by a dear person who is ruining his life, and tragically wrecking the lives of those who love him. Reduced to human semi-impotence, and to tears, one must implore God to give us belief in the prodigal son, after he has sunk so low. For Jesus Christ there are no lost people. Whatever their behaviour he believes in everyone, for he sees them with different eyes from ours - eyes which penetrate to their innermost hearts, where they were begotten by their Father's loving breath. He believes in them, because he knows that, suffering for and with them, he has saved them all.

Without neglecting the human means suggested by intelligence, if we join with Jesus Christ in looking at people, especially those of whom we despair, we will help them to renew their lives.

Here I am this evening, Lord, with you,
 with him,
 with her.
He is my son,
 my wife,
 my granddaughter
 or my friend - it doesn't matter!
He is a poor lost, big child,
a ship with broken moorings,
in the storm of life.
 He is adrift,
 drugged,
 alcoholic,
 debauched and a liar,
 sometimes violent,
 loathesome …

He is greedy,
   insatiable,
burning with a furious desire to live,
and sometimes with a throbbing desire to die,
to die because he can't manage to live.
   He is searching,
   searching for what?
   For pleasure.
   What pleasure?
   For happiness.
   What happiness?
   He doesn't know.
   He doesn't know any more.
His body is broken, and his heart is torn apart.

All around him, the desert.
Those who know him have one by one been disheartened.
   They weep.
The right thinking ones have condemned him:
   a contagious sick person to be avoided,
   or else imprisoned.
But, Lord, I love him,
and can't bring myself to leave him to die.
   He is my big boy,
   my big girl …
   my little boy …
   my little girl …
and in spite of his failing and failing again,
in spite of my fears and despair,
   in spite of everything,
   I continue to believe in him.

Many times,
looking at him in his degenerate state
I have exclaimed in front of *him*:

"You are wonderful"!
   He has started
with a hint of doubt,
but also a gleam
lighting up his eyes for a moment,
      and once ...
oh precious, minute hope in the darkness!
when I was clumsily reproaching him for his way of life,
      he murmured,
      weeping,
      distraught:
'All this isn't me!'

It's true, Lord,
isn't it true!
It isn't *him*,
      I believe it.
      I want to believe it.
      but make my faith grow,
      my faith in *him*,
      my faith in you who call me,
      prove me each day,
      through him.
Grant me to believe that it is God,
      our Father,
who at this moment imparts to him a breath of life
      as yesterday,
and as tomorrow he will offer it to him again,
accompanying him faithfully on his lost way.
Grant me to believe that he is like all men
      made in your image every day,
underneath his horrible mask
and the mud of the journey.

155

Grant me to believe
that you, in the terrifying night of your passion, long ago,
    you saved him.

Grant me to believe then,
that today,
    in spite of everything
    and perhaps in spite of himself
    at the bottom of his heart,
this heart buried in a tomb sealed with a stone,
    this child of God is moving,
    growing,
    wanting to be born,
and that to rise again he only needs
a loving look to draw him
and a voice speaking to him
as yours did long ago
to the heart of the sinful woman:
"*I will not condemn you …*"
because I love you
and because I have faith in you.

Grant me, Lord,
    I beseech you,
to be the one who says it to him
    and who believes in him,
    who believes him with all my soul
    since you believe in him.

Judge not …	*Matthew 7 v 1-2*
Love your enemies …	*Matthew 5 vv 44-45*
They that are whole need not a physician.	*Luke 5 30-31*

XXXII
She said to him: "I shall be with you, my child".

Jesus Christ is present in our lives. We are told so, repeatedly. We believe faintly, deeply. But whether we are at the beginning of our relationship with him, or deeply engaged in a lifetime of friendship with him, we always suffer from not seeing, not touching him.

We have to understand that "physical" presence isn't the whole presence of the people we meet. Those who really love each other know this from experience. It is love which makes people truly aware of each other and the intensity of this love matches the intensity of their mutual awareness. God who loves us all infinitely is present to each one of us as a complete presence.

Formerly morning and evening prayers started with the words: "Let us bring ourselves into the presence of God and let us adore Him". If we get into the habit of often bringing ourselves into the presence of God during the day, our life will be transformed.

The man was leaving, Lord, I don't know where he was going,
setting out for some important part of his life – I don't know what.
Leaning over his old mother,
he embraced her tenderly,
and she
embraced him even more tenderly,
then holding his face between her trembling hands,
she murmured:
'Go, my child, I shall be with you'.
There was a long silence …
then she added:
'Do you believe me?'
'Yes, mother', he said.

He left.
And she,
with her tearful gaze,
accompanied him from afar.
Later on the man told me,
that on each of his distant journeys
it was thus,
and that at difficult moments,
    believing that his mother
    was accompanying him with her love,
    gave him strength.

    And I, this evening,
    meditating,
    suddenly realise, Lord,
that these are the same words
    that you said
    when you took leave of us,
    to return to the Father,
'I shall be with you … till the end of time.'
And I am sure that you expect the same response from us,
    as the son to his mother,
    "Yes, we believe you".

Lord, you know that I am weak
    and often,
    at difficult moments
I seek a friendly presence to sustain me.
    I need a word,
    a hand to press,
    a face to kiss.
But now I have understood

that a physical presence
does not necessarily mean a real presence.
     Two beings can see each other,
     touch each other
     and even embrace very warmly,
     but remain distant,
     very distant from each other,
     separated,
     if their love,
     in their innermost hearts
     does not unite them.
How many clasped hands are only a mockery?
How many couples,
who have long slept together in the same bed from habit
are no more than two solitary people
camping on one side and the other
of an impassable gulf!

     But I also believe, Lord,
     with all my heart,
That two beings who have cruelly drifted apart from each other,
     because of space or time,
     can join up again,
     unite,
     live in deep communion,
     if their love is alive.

I believe it of people, Lord,
how then not to believe it of you
     since you love us *infinitely*.
     Your presence with all of us
     must be *infinite*,

real presence,
        total presence,
        everywhere and forever.
Nothing can separate us from you,
nothing which comes from you,
only what comes from us,
        and above all ...
        our lack of faith.

This evening, Lord,
        you tell me again:
'I shall be with you till the end of time!'
        And you ask me quietly:
'Do you believe me?'
        Yes, Lord, I believe you,
        but help my unbelief.

Grant me always to live
in your loving presence,
you who accompany me on my daily round,
        just as that old mother
        accompanies her son with her faithful love.
Help me to work *in your presence,*
        to enjoy myself *in your presence,*
        to relax *in your presence,*
for if I think that you are there, Lord,
if I open my heart to your love which you offer,
        I shall never again be alone,
        never again be weak.
And before you I could no longer
        do the wrong which I want to do,
        not like the little child
        who is afraid that his mother will see him

and is afraid of being punished,
but like the grown-up son
who, realising his mother's immense love,
only wants one thing in his life:
    to give her thanks.

I will behold thy face ... and I shall be satisfied with thy likeness.

Psalm 17 v i5

Who will separate us from the love of Christ?

Romans 8 vv 35 & 38-39

Lord my heart is .... is like a little child with his mother.

Psalm 131

I will walk before the Lord in the land of the living.

Psalm 116 v 9

XXXIII
LORD, I HAVEN'T YET KNOWN JOY.

Pleasure is relatively easy to get. In its various forms it is above all food for the body. But usually this food is very quickly consumed and often leaves a vague taste of dissatisfaction.
Joy is our soul's guest. It is difficult to acquire. It is virtue which takes possession of us and it is an incomprehensible mystery for those who haven't experienced it. It can coexist in the same heart, with great suffering. God alone is perfect happiness, perfect joy. Only people of a pure heart, in spite of the pain of glimpsing on earth only a few gleams of the beauty and majesty of God, and in spite of the sorrow of seeing their brothers and sisters suffer, can attain this joy by opening themselves to God, and receiving it from him. Isn't it the property of the saints ...? But can we truly say that 'we have become completely familiar with JOY'?

Lord, we are told that one must smile,
    smile every day
    and smile again.
We are told that joy is a solid Christian virtue
    and that a sad saint
    is a bad saint.
I am told that no-one bears witness to you
    if his face and his life
do not radiate your joy.
I want to believe it ...
but, Lord, I haven't yet
    known joy.

For me joy is too often an inconstant visitor,
    it flees,
    returns,

only to depart again.
At the moment when at last I believe I have caught it for a
moment
   it disappears,
and into the blue sky of my heart
   a few clouds drift,
   and sometimes the clouds
   explode into storms ...
   rain falls on my joy.

Lord,
if I haven't yet known joy,
   it is your fault!
You told me that all men are my brothers
   and that I must love them all,
   even my enemies.
I have tried, I try, and sometimes I think I have succeeded.
But then I have found, Lord,
   that when I love
   I must accept suffering,
   the sufferings of those whom one loves...
and often their suffering is immense!

Lord,
I don't understand.
Can one be completely happy?
when in the emptiness of peaceful days,
   or in the silence of the night,
haunting groans,
rending cries
beset us persistently
   in the muttered protests of strikers,
   in the moans of the famished,
the tears of separated couples and lost children,
   the death rattles of the dying,

the screams of the tortured,
the appalling tumult of battles ...
an atrocious, immeasurable, discordant concert
which rises up to us
unceasingly
from this vast, torn humanity,
members of a body which struggling, bleeding, you wanted to
be united and happy.

Lord,
I don't understand,
your apostle Paul said:
*When one member suffers
all members suffer with him*',
and I would suffer more
if I loved more,
but I would stop suffering, I believe,
if my brothers and sisters stopped groaning.

No, I can never be completely happy
when so many members of my family
are unhappy ...

Some people can manage it, Lord.
At table, they say, watching television
and the horrific images
that it puts out every day:
'It's horrible!'
And then after an embarrassed silence;
'What have we got for pudding today?'
Opening the newspaper,
and finding the headline, they exclaim:
'Another outrage and innocent people killed.
It's appalling!'
And then, a minute later:

'There's a very funny film on television on Sunday,
    we must watch it!'
They declare during a serious meeting:
    "*What should be done, is ...*"
    so much that will not be done ...
They will talk about it for two hours ...
then, before going to bed,
    have a friendly drink together,
    laughing and telling good stories.
They pray regularly,
good Christians, in universal prayer,
for all the many, varied unfortunates
    and then sing of their joy at being together
    with you
and at being able to offer your saving sacrifice to the Father.
Again they say:
'one must enjoy life!
Its not a sin to be happy
its unhealthy to feel guilty
and even more to blame others,
one has already given enough!
people must have faith!
Jesus is Lord, he is risen!
    Let us sing, embrace, be happy!'

They say ...
they say,
    and I too, Lord, say,
    I too live,
    I too laugh,
but some day I fear
    that my joy is a ready-made joy,
    a noisy burst of laughter
    to cover up the wails of mankind.
I am afraid that my joy

is born of an easily appeased conscience,
    satisfied with a few donations,
    and with some good works.
I am afraid that my momentary joy is in sleep,
    evasion in golden dreams,
born in the illusion of a deep faith.
…Lord, I have not yet known Joy!

Lord,
if I haven't yet known joy,
    it's also because …
you have created us too small
    for your joy which is too great for us.
Can one be completely happy,
    when in our bodies and our hearts,
    we are tortured by some hunger
    that we can only relieve
    but never satisfy?
Can one be completely happy,
    when life laughs us to scorn every morning
    with a vision of impossible dreams
    which by evening have never been realised?
    Can one be completely happy
    when shaking a hand,
    brushing lips,
    only lets us skim over the hidden mystery
    of the other being with us.

Can one be completely happy
    when your face
    glimpsed in prayer on some days,
    is then hidden
in the overlong darkness of days.
…Lord, I haven't yet known joy!

My child, says the Lord,
accept your limits,
     you are not God,
     you aren't *everything,*
but you are a member of my body
     and each member receives
     some little bits of joy,
     like a mouthful of nourishing bread,
     like a sip of refreshing wine.
Receive them.
I give them to you.

But it is true, my child,
     that if I am for and with you all,
     living, risen,
equally I am, in my members,
     crucified every day.
My passion is not completed
     while my children suffer
And you suffer with *me.*
It is the disciple's lot,
     I foretold it to you.

Do not be ashamed of suffering
but do what you have to do
     for your brothers and sisters
     around you
     generously,
then you will know peace,
my peace,
that which I promised you:
     'I leave you my peace,
     I give you my peace'.

As for the joy that you ask for,
      complete and total joy,
perhaps you will have to wait for the day
when I shall say to you:
'*Well done, good and faithful servant
enter into the joy of your master*'.

Jesus said...Take no thought for your life, what ye shall eat. But rather
seek ye the kingdom of God. *Luke 12 vv 22-23 & 31-32*

"I love you as my Father loves me..." *John 15 vv 9-11*

XXXIV
LORD, THEY ARE IN LOVE, THOSE TWO.

People communicate and express their friendship and their love by their bodies, words and gestures. The handclasp and above all the lover's kiss are wonderful "signs" when they are authentic. Unfortunately people do not always put the whole of themselves into these gestures, which should be 'a human sacrament'. Then they deceive, sometimes even betray.

God also assumed a body. He revealed himself in human words; he expressed his friendship and; affection with human gestures. But he put his whole self into his words and gestures: 'only say a word and I shall be healed'. In his Church he continues to give himself wholly through words and gestures: the sacraments.

If our gestures of friendship and love were sincere and if Christ were fully within us, we could, through them, express to our brothers and sisters something of the loving goodness of God, of him who, in order to be with us, was made flesh.

Lord they are in love, those two.
> I know it.
> You know it.
They kissed in front of me.
> I saw them.
> You saw them.
And we were happy, weren't we?
For a kiss is beautiful, Lord,
when it's a sacrament of love,
> a whispered exchange:
'I give you my life and I accept yours.'
> Lips meet:
'I offer myself as food and you satisfy me'.
> So lovers

exchange messages,
attempt to realise their dream of being one.
Yes, it is beautiful, Lord,
for they are in love.
today in your light
they have shown it one to the other,
and very quietly
I have thanked you for our bodies
which, without a word,
can convey 'I love you,'
to all those one loves.
For you have given us bodies, Lord,
and hands
and lips
to express our beating hearts
which can't express themselves.
Our souls without bodies would be silent indeed
and our love trapped,
and without bodies nothing would be known,
neither the other's love
nor its tenderness.

And you too, my God,
ineffable mystery,
you so great,
so distant,
so inaccessible,
that no one has seen you at any time   *John 1 18*
nor heard
nor touched you,
one day
you became flesh
for us,
and through your son,

your Word became flesh,
and proclaimed to us your infinite love.
You, Jesus,
    who long ago were hungrily fed
    with the milk of Mary's breast,
    a mother like us,
you who later on,
    laying your hands on the sick,
    gave them back health
    and gave them your life,
you who let yourself be touched
    by the crowd of rich and poor alike,
    of good men and robbers,
    of adulterers,
    of prostitutes ...
you who caressed sinners,
    hugged children,
you who by your crucifixion
    crucified our sins,
you who offered that body to all people
    as an effective *sign*,
    a sublime kiss of love
    to the person who receives it,
    food of *life*
    union in common
    communion.
Finally you who no longer have flesh today,
    nor hands
    or lips
    to tell your love,
    but who, through ours,
    still want quietly to tell it to everyone,
I beg you,
    teach us to love with this rebellious body,

a body created to express our tenderness
and to *make* love,
but which often, alas,
too gross and too greedy,
seeks to be fed more than to give,
expressing our needs more than our true self.
Forgive us for all those signs of friendship,
of affection or love,
which too often are deceitful masks
with no life behind them
when they aren't lies,
and deliberate deception
of those who receive them,
and those who watch.
Forgive us for those automatic handclasps,
distributed in the course of the day
without even exchanging a fleeting glance.
For those clasps which seek attention
in the clamour of voices,
while faking interest.
For those deceitful clasps,
mockeries of friendship,
when the heart rejects,
but the body pretends.
Forgive us above all,
for those stolen kisses grabbed by surprise,
for those greedy kisses
only seeking pleasure,
for those cheating kisses
concealing breakdown of relationship,
and those debauched, banal kisses,
self centred,
wasted,
empty of affection

and of love.
Oh yes, my God,
    teach me to love with this rebellious body!
Tomorrow, Lord, if you don't help me,
        I will set out again on my daily round.
        I don't know where my heart and soul
        will be wandering,
I am so often absent from my body,
        its voice is false,
        its songs of love
        out of tune.
With all my strength
        this evening once again,
I beg you,
        wash my hands and purify my lips,
        so often prostituted.
Open my soul to your infinite love,
        and re-unite my body and my heart
        which are so often separated.
Then, rich in myself and enriched by you,
        I will be close to others
and through my loving gestures
I will tell them something
of your love made *flesh*.

Do you not know that your bodies are members of Christ made flesh. *1 Corinthians 6 v 15 & vv 19-20*

The Word became flesh. *John 1 v 14*

A Pharisee invited Jesus to dine with him. *Luke 7 vv 36-38*

XXXV
He clasped me tightly and said to me: "I adore you!"

Many Christians take the Lord's commandment, "Love your brothers and sisters" seriously. But some approach it with their heads. That is to say they do fraternal acts as their mind tells them. They have no spontaneity for the hungry one. They perform a "task". Now, not only children but all people need friendship, to feel tenderness. They lack it so much. We should approach other people with our whole being, body, heart and mind together and not just with part of ourselves, and Jesus, who let himself be "touched", to be embraced and who knew how to embrace, could, through us, continue to reach people with "a heart of flesh".

A little child, Lord,
    an abandoned child
that a loving family took into their warm home.
He is marked by his past sufferings
    and his face
    cries out for tenderness.

I tried to look at him,
    as I believe
    you would have looked at him.
I smiled at him, I listened to him,
and in a few moments
we were in touch.
    Suddenly
    he jumped into my wide open arms,
    he hugged me tightly and said to me;
    "I adore you!"
and with the same fervour I said to him;
    "I too".

My mother used to say, one only adores God'
    and, I don't know why,
I remembered it at that moment.
But this evening I dare to think, Lord,
    that through me the child,
    and I through him,
    together,
we discovered and reached something of you.

For you suffer with him, Lord,
    and through him,
    and his cry is your cry,
    and I believe
    I heard it this morning.

Lord,
I would like to be at the feet of the crucified child,
as at the foot of the cross.
But I would also like the child,
taken down at last from the dead wood
where evil has nailed him,
to be able to find and be *touched* by a little of your love
in my arms which are full of tenderness.

I have so longed, Lord,
to gather my whole being together,
to approach people
    with the riches of my whole life,
refusing to live with my head alone,
    that arid response to the commandment of love,
but fearing to love with my sensitive heart alone
or my greedy body.
Help me Lord,
to gather within me

what is fragmented,
to unify my strengths, and to risk offering the starving
    my living heart
    from which they may be nourished,
    and not just a few wisely programmed gestures of charity.

Help me to be opened wide to your brotherly love,
    so that, being in touch with my life,
    they are a little in touch
    with yours.
For, Lord, you no longer have
arms to receive the children of the earth,
    above all those who are rejected,
    as formerly the apostles rejected
    those who crossed your path.
You no longer have knees for them to sit on,
    words to speak to them,
    and to make them laugh,
    and finally lips
    to kiss them tenderly.
But marvellously you wanted
    us to be needed,
    me to be needed
    as a poor mirror,
    to reflect a few beams of your love.

This evening, Lord, I thank you
    for having been able this morning
to offer you a little of myself, *living,*
    to reach the child
    who was secretly trying to get near
    and to touch you.
But forgive me, Lord,
for having so often wasted,

or kept to myself,
    what I should have given to others.
For if it is often easy for me
to refuse nothing to a child,
it is, alas, difficult for me to give and give of myself
    to *all* my companions on the journey.

And yet, Lord, I know that every man
    is a child
    who goes on growing until he is dead,
And whether he is small or big,
    with a pure or disfigured face,
    he is God's child
    waiting for his love.

Jesus took a child and set him in the midst of them.
Mark 9 vv 36–37

Yes God is my record how greatly I long after you all in the bowels of
Christ. *Philippians 1 v 8*

But we were gentle among you, even as a nurse cherisheth her children.
1 Thessalonians 2 vv 7–8

XXXVI
PRAYER FOR MY UNKNOWN BROTHERS AND SISTERS.

Whether we like it or not we are all brothers and sisters. But the human family is numerous and there are many frontiers of all kinds which have divided us from each other and often we make enemies.
The task of rediscovering our unknown brothers, of forming links with them and of again making a family of scattered peoples is the only human plan. Jesus came for that purpose. He asked us to love all our brothers and sisters as ourselves and as he himself loved us. He gave his life for us so that we should do this. Those who accept it, become 'children of God' in him. Together they can, whatever their race, their social class, their behaviour ... turn to God calling him 'our' Father. There are no more outsiders.

Is it true, O my God,
that always,
even before we became men,
    standing upright on the planet,
even before the universe itself
    emerged from nothing,
you, in your infinite love,
thought and dreamed of each one of us?

Is it true that always,
even before your son,
    your Word,
    came to us,
even before it was announced
    by the prophets,
you saw *us* in *him*
    and already
    loved us all as your children?
Is it true that at the beginning of the world

you gave this earth
    not just to a few people but to all,
an unique land for many coloured faces
to live in together
    and together to transform it?

Is it true that, when Jesus came,
    like us a man,
    he welcomed us all as brothers,
    unconditionally,
carrying us in his heart,
    so far,
    so profoundly,
that we were incorporated in him
    becoming members of his body,
    to the point that
    we couldn't touch any one of us
without his saying, 'It is I'?

Finally is it true
    that in him, who has overcome death,
with him we have entered the resurrection
and have been invited to live forever with our Father
    as a united family,
    loving him and ourselves
    as they who are with him love?

If it is true, Oh my God,
    and I believe it is,
how can we call a single person a stranger
since we are all children of the same Father,
    and brothers and sisters one with another?
...and by what means dare we then,
    (oh my God forgive us!)
decide that such or such land
    is forever ours

and that one must have a visa to enter it,
that that job was reserved for us
    unless we reject it
    as unworthy of us,
that this man deserves to be accepted,
    while that one,
    should be banished far away.
How can we do it, my God,
    without tearing your family apart,
seriously mutilating the body of your son,
    and in mutilating it,
    mortally wound ourselves?

Forgive us, my God, but understand,
when you gave us the earth it was so huge for us,
    who are so small,
    that we have grown
    far apart from each other.

We have developed different colours,
    different languages,
    diverse customs.
We have made false gods for ourselves,
    often in ignorance that we have only one,
    and that this is God the Father.
Finally, nowadays,
when we can all know each other
    and even visit each other,
when someone appears among us
whom we haven't already met,
    how can we remain indifferent or hostile,
    and call him a *stranger*...
    instead of bounding with joy,
happy to be able to embrace an *unknown brother*?
Nonetheless, oh our Father,
    it is by these glad reunions

which you have always dreamed of,
and of which your Son told us
that we shall be judged.
Whether we know it or not,
that unknown brother *is He*...   *Matthew 25 31-46*

My God, I know it and I am ashamed of knowing it,
    and not living what I know.
For if I proclaim loudly,
    sometimes passionately,
    in superficial discussions:
"*I am not a racist!*"
I often think to myself:
that all the same there are limits ...
    that it is our duty to preserve ...
    that given the circumstances ...,
and I find that rigid frontiers still exist
    in my heart.

Oh my God, help me!
Help me to change my selfish heart
    into a brotherly heart,
    so that no-one may ever be
    excluded from my company.
Help me to respect people who are different,
    without wanting to make them in my image,
while remaining proudly convinced,
    that that image
    is the right kind.
Help me on the contrary
    to see myself as small and poor,
before my brothers and sisters who so little resemble me,
    so that I may be enriched
    by their differences.
Help me to seize every opportunity of meeting people
    which nowadays happens so often,

that I may be torn out of myself
and, approaching others,
    make neighbours of those who were far off.

Help me not to judge, even less to condemn,
    those who in their lives
    have serious trouble with these diverse brothers and sisters.
Help me to be clear-headed in difficulties
    and without denying the problems,
    to fight them where I am,
    with whatever means I have
    so that
    rules and laws
    are never made,
which prevent us from meeting
    with unknown brothers and sisters.
Finally, help me to be more open to the life of your son every day,
    for I believe,
    it is that *life*
    which makes us brothers.
And then, oh my God,
    as a faithful worker in your loving plan
    I shall be able to say, every evening,
    when saying goodnight to you,
    'Our Father'.

He who loves his brother abideth in the light.   *1 John 2 vv 10-11*

You are all sons of God, by faith, in Christ Jesus.
    Galatians 3 vv 26-28

XXXVII
LORD, I AM INCAPABLE OF "GIVING MY WHOLE LIFE" PIECE BY PIECE.

One throws away what is useless. So we want our lives to be useful to those we love, but also to all our brothers and sisters if possible. There is so much to do on this earth where suffering, in its many forms, crushes thousands of people. Who hasn't dreamed of 'giving' their whole life to others and to the Lord. But we come up hard against our limits and very quickly resign ourselves, thinking that total generosity is reserved for heroes and saints. What most alarms us is constancy. Is it possible to offer every day, every moment of our life? Humanly speaking, no. With Christ, yes, for we can give him everything; the best of ourselves, the less good and even sin. And he can make an offering of the fullness but also of the failings of our life.

Lord, I believe
that I would be capable of doing
some extraordinary deed
   ...once in a while.
A deed which would mobilise my whole being,
    because I was shocked by misery,
    because I was revolted by an injustice,
    because one of my own was in danger.
on some days I even believe
that I would be capable of risking my life,
    I see myself giving it
    in one go,
for my ideals,
for my love,
for my child
   ...and perhaps even someone else's child.
And if, alas, this thought,

183

secretly,
allows me to admire myself a little,
   equally it reassures me.
For you have said to us, Lord,
   that to give one's life for others,
is the greatest possible proof of love.

But what humiliates me,
   and often discourages me,
is that I am incapable of *giving my life*
   piece by piece,
   every little piece,
   day after day,
   hour by hour,
   minute by minute,
   to give
   always to give,
   ...and to give *myself.*
I cannot do this,
and yet surely this is what you ask of me.

What you ask of me is so simple, Lord!
   It's too simple,
   ...and too difficult.
Every day to do what I have to do,
   a little step, then another,
   and next day, yet another
   on my daily round.
Every day to journey with those near to me,
   my husband, my wife, my children,
   my colleagues at work,
   my neighbours,
   and the many people I encounter.
Every day and every moment,

to struggle to live
as you want me to live,
and with others to battle
so that all men can live as human beings.
Every day to give a thousand small bits of my life,
in a thousand possible loving gestures,
which are no longer noticed,
because they are so ordinary
but which you tell me that you need
in order to weave together an offering,
and so that one day, I can truly say:
I have given my whole life to my brothers.

That's what you want, Lord,
...but I can't do it.

Why have you invented constancy, Lord,
and fidelity in small things
and love which is endless in its demands!
I have dreamt of giving my whole life to another,
one other,
and to many,
and, unknowing, I imagined
that one could achieve this with a single yes
a single gesture,
a single offering.
But I have found that thousands are needed,
perhaps millions.
I dreamt of a life blazing
with a few great deeds,
and very quickly
I got to know that it must be lived
very slowly,
fed continually with minute twigs

which keep the flame from going out.
Always to start again,
>   *always.*
Lord, I can't do it,
>   and I know it
>   and I'm afraid
>   that when I come before you
and bring my life into your Light
>   I will find that, apart from a few given moments,
I will have refused thousands
…and I will not have given my whole life …
>   but only
>   a few pieces of it.

It is true, my child, says the Lord,
>   that it happens
that some people are allowed
to give up all their light,
>   in a few sparkling flashes,
but many are asked
>   to light up a thousand small loving lights
>   in the profound darkness of their time.
>   Do not regret.
>   Do not judge.
For who can say that millions of candles
lit in the course of a long life,
do not make a bigger light
than a showy firework?
For the rest, my child,
I don't ask you always to succeed,
>   but always to try.
And above all, listen to me.
I ask you to *accept in the end your limits,,*
to recognise your poverty, and to give it to me,

for to give your life,
is not only to give your wealth,
  but your poverty also,
  and even your sins.
Do this, my child,
I will fill in the holes left by the little bits of wasted life
  which you subtracted from all the rest,
and I will restore wholeness to you.
  For in my hands
  the poverty you offer will become wealth,
  ... for eternity ...

Whoever would save his life will lose it ...   *Mark 8 vv 34-37*

God who is rich in mercy ... has quickened us again in Christ.
Ephesians 2 vv 4-6

XXXVIII
We haven't stopped loving each other.

Nothing is crueller for a married couple, who have loved and been together for many years, than to be parted by death. Nonetheless they haven't stopped loving each other, for the departed loved one is living another life beyond death and love cannot die when it is authentic love in Christ.

But to love, without the physical presence of the loved one is a terrible trial, a 'purgatory': the final purification of love before being reunited in eternity. Happy is he then, who remains faithful when left alone on this earth and continues to live in the twilight of his or her love, which certainly doesn't mean that 'remaking one's life', in popular language, is to be unfaithful. He can pass on to his children, and to everyone who doubts the possibility of love, or even doesn't know what it is to love, proof that love can endure and flourish without two bodies travelling side by side, happily and as one, and that finally its radiance is freely seen; 'I suffer from the absence of the loved one, but I am happy that he is happy'.

As for such tenderness, may it help all who need it!

I woke up, Lord,
    ...and he wasn't there any more.
I turned over in my bed
    ...but it was empty,
and my lonely fingers still sought his.

My love is with you;
    I know it, I hope it,
but Lord, I cannot get used
    to his absence,
and every awakening is anguish for me,
    like the anguish
    of a sick person awakening to his amputated limbs.

He is no longer there!
I will hear it no more, my song that is you.
No longer will I be the background
    for his everyday work.
No more will I trace the wrinkled furrows
    on his beloved face,
    from which I glean life,
    where day after day,
    in joy and in sorrow,
    we sowed
    and harvested
    a thousand fruits of love.
No more will I seek, in the depths of his eyes,
the soft light of his tranquil gaze,
    after the bright mornings,
    the midday fire,
    and sometimes the shadowed days
    when clouds gathered
    and the storm burst,
before the rainbow of peace
rose in our hearts.

We loved each other, Lord,
we haven't stopped loving each other!

Lord, we were in love,
and we lived close together,
he in me and I in him.
and you,
    you sealed our two lives,
    to make them as one.
But he has gone to those distant shores,
    that no one reaches
    except by passing through death,
and from my side, my feet still on this earth,

I cannot even see him,
  oh my beloved ... vanished,
  far away,
  so far,
  in the mists of infinity,
  he isn't here any more!

They say one gets used to it, Lord,
that time does its work,
  but I know now
  that neither time nor death can overcome love,
  for I murmured one morning, 'Always'
  and he said to me, 'Always',
  and you promised us
that we would love each other till eternity!
  Without seeing him, Lord,
  I want to believe it,
  I do believe it.
  We haven't stopped loving each other!

But yesterday we embarked
  on every day together,
for, if the one sought happiness for the other,
  we often found it for ourselves.
Sometimes we gave and sometimes we took,
  but our continual efforts
  increased our love.

Today we have entered purgatory.
  I suffer for being alone,
  he suffers for being far away,
  for can he be happy without me
  when I am unhappy without him!
But, Lord, in your light,
he is purifying our love,

while I
   must perfect it
   in the dark.
Help me, O Lord,
to love him today in his absence
      even more
      than in his presence yesterday,
In fact to love him for himself, without seeking any return,
      happy that he is happy
      to be near you,
      not receiving anything for myself
      except the joy of his Joy.

Yes, my love lives undiminished in my heart,
      death can do nothing about it;
      and there's my pain.
for the springs of my heart have not dried up, Lord,
      they flow and overflow,
and I have an abundance of loving words,
      and a thousand tender gestures,
unused smiles in reserve,
and a rain of tears which flood my heart,
      and make all those flowers of love
      grow even faster.

Lord, I will not let them
      wilt,
      or fade,
      in my enclosed heart,
every day I will gather them,
a marvellous harvest for my children,
      and my grandchildren,
      my friends
      and neighbours
      and all those forgotten beggars

who seek wisps of love
at my roadside.
But my pain, Lord,
my pain remains!
The dreadful loneliness, and the long days
and the dark nights,
the absence,
cruel absence,
The profound emptiness into which on some evenings,
my heart, driven crazy, plunges to a bottomless pit.
I miss him, Lord, do you understand?
I miss him!
Why have you abandoned me?

Forgive me, Lord,
forgive me for my times of despair,
you, who every day speak to us from your cross.
It is when I forget to look at you
that darkness invades me.
You wait for me
and from near you he looks at me,
and draws me in with his love,
guides and sustains me.

Thanks to thee, Lord,
and thanks to him
my very pain will not be wasted,
For I will offer this abundance of love
which my pain demands of me,
love which lives and increases beyond my pain.
I will offer it for those young explorers in love
who seek without finding,
losing themselves,
innocents,
in the illusions of a moment.

Those, Lord, who don't know
what it is to love,
  what it is to tear oneself apart to give to another
  and open oneself wide to receive the gift of the other.
Those who don't know
that love is very often painful
  before becoming joy,
joy of a new life which takes flesh
  in the two lives united
  without ever destroying each other.
Those who don't know
that there is no love which isn't for always,
  and that you alone can give
  an infinite dimension to this love.

I would like to tell them about it, Lord,
  through my life to tell them,
  and since my beloved awaits me,
  I will also await
  our meeting in peace.
and from this new commitment,
  cruel and sweet commitment,
I will make an offering of this waiting time
until, at last, in the arms of my beloved
  we will love each other,
  Lord,
  as we do with you,
  infinitely, eternally.

But if Christ is not risen our preaching is in vain …
1 Corinthians 15 v 14 vv 16-19

Let not your heart be troubled … *John 14 vv 1-3*

XXXIX
I WILL LET MYSELF BE TAKEN IN YOUR ARMS, LORD!

There are many 'expressions of faith' which, used and repeated without any explanation, are very inept and sometimes false, especially those concerning suffering. Certainly, the Christians who use them are sincere, and, one must hope, find a profound meaning in the inexact words, but for non-believers who are put off by formulas, they are repellent. Many people have been repelled from the 'good' God presented in this way, who seemed monstrous to them.

Suffering is always bad, a 'rubbish dump'. God does not enjoy it, he 'puts up' with it. But he hasn't left us alone with this suffering. Jesus Christ has salvaged the rubbish. Bearing his own sufferings, he has borne ours with them. He has made of them 'the primary matter of redemption'. But, mind you, Jesus Christ didn't save 'by his sufferings', but by the love with which he bore his sufferings and ours. Only love can save and only love gives life. In the face of suffering we must first fight with all our strength to reduce it. When it can't be avoided in our lives, let us pray to the Lord for the power to be joined with him. He has already suffered our sufferings. May we then consciously let ourselves be carried by him, enduring our trials with him. May we then, in the darkness, not 'offer our suffering' - one doesn't offer rubbish - but offer our faith in his saving love.

I was watching them, Lord …
two little friends,
but they had a fight today.
They fell down,
    and they were both slightly hurt,
    they cried,
    and sobbed,
    and …
the two mothers came running.

One tried to take her child in her arms
but the child, stamping, pushed her away, beaten.
  He remained alone,
  shut in,
  enclosed,
  and still crying.
The other let himself be swept up
in a whirlwind of love.
  His mother covered him with kisses.
  His tears dried up.
From time to time he smiled, saying:
  'I'm sore, I'm sore'.
He was the one more hurt.

  Lord,
some people say that God
loves those more who suffer more.
  It's not true is it?
You cannot love anyone more or less,
since you love each one of us individually,
  and everyone *infinitely,*
  but when we suffer,
  your love,
  like that of a tender mother,
  is *nearer,*
more available.
And like those little children
  we can let you carry us,
  and bear our sufferings with us,
  or else repel you
and remain alone, overwhelmed, in revolt.

So great suffering
  can bring us nearer God,
or distance us from him.

There are many who distance themselves, Lord, …
they haven't believed in your love.
And perhaps even more
than those who suffer themselves,
there are many who impotently
watch those they love suffering cruelly.
    And I,
    proud,
    sure of myself,
    I say that I believe!

But it is easy for me to say so,
I am not suffering
    and I know
that if one day
I am crucified by great pain,
    I will implore,
    cry out,
    and perhaps like the hurt child I too
    will rebel.

Then, Lord, will I accuse you? …
As if you wanted suffering
    and imposed it on us:
    you, who want us to be happy,
    and give us life.

Perhaps I will ask myself:
what have I done to deserve these trials?
as if you were punishing us,
    like teachers who lack authority
    and punish their pupils,
    like fathers who make themselves heard or respected
    and compensate for *their* imperfections
    with their severity.

As if we didn't punish ourselves enough
    and you needed to add to it,
    like parents who slap their disobedient
    children's faces
    when they fall and are hurt …
    and suffer.

Shall I perhaps demand a miracle from you?
as if you didn't give all men
the freedom,
    to run their own lives,
    to fight against all the world's evils,
    to battle with sin,
    which mysteriously,
    remorselessly,
rots the world
and causes immeasurable sufferings.

Shall I perhaps treat you as insensitive,
you, the *good* God?
as if you didn't suffer
    seeing us suffering,
as everyone who loves, suffers
    when they see loved ones suffering.

Since, Lord, today I can turn to you,
with hands and heart free of the bonds of suffering
    I beseech you,
    I beg you,
beyond the pious and false thoughts
    which bring some of the faithful on to their knees,
    but which make so very many of our brothers and sisters
    seethe with indignation,
    enlighten me!

Then, when in great distress one day,
perhaps I shall understand
that suffering in itself
is never a grace,
    never.
For it is a rubbish heap,
    rubbish of an imperfect world,
    and imperfect humanity,
    because people are only creatures
    and they had to be redeemed by you,
    recreated.

Perhaps I shall understand
    that you,
    Jesus,
    didn't bless your suffering,
    accept it as a gift,
that you didn't *seek* it,
    but *endured* it.

For, oh Jesus,
your cross fell on you!
    The cross on your shoulders.
    You, on the cross.
    Attached.
    Nailed.
    Unable to escape.
    You, crucified, body and soul,
    helpless,
    trembling with fear and pain,
    you cried out,
begging your Father to do a miracle ...
    and he didn't do it ...

He couldn't do it,
for does a father prevent his son
from enduring right to the end
in solidarity with his brothers!

I ask you then that I may believe
with all my strength
that you didn't come to relieve our sufferings
but, having helped us to fight *against* them,
    to live through them with us.
For in those days, Jesus,
    you bore not only your cross, but ours,
    the great ones and the small,
    those from yesterday,
    today,
    tomorrow,
    those of the whole of humanity,,
    since you love us.
    and as *victim* of your love,
all human suffering
has become your suffering.
Oh great and loving Jesus,
your love was needed to carry all those crosses
    right to the end.
Your infinite love was needed
    to raise them up,
    to erect them,
your body raised above the earth,
your heart raised to the sky.
All the power of your love was needed
    to embody them,
    burn them,
    dissolve them
    and liberate *life*.

For it isn't dead wood
which gives warmth and light,
    it's the flame.
It isn't dead wood which must be offered,
    but the *fire,*
    the *fire* of *love* which burns up everything.
    It is done.
    All is done.
Suffering and death are vanquished!

But, Lord, today I am not suffering! ...
    and if, tomorrow,
    I can do nothing else ...
    except suffer,
give me, I beseech you in advance,
the courage to offer
my powerlessness.
And, like the hurt child,
let myself be taken in your arms
    and your love will carry me
    into eternity!

Let no man say when he is tempted, 'I am tempted by God'.
                                        James 1 vv 13-15

Surely he has borne our griefs and carried our sorrows.
                                        Isaiah 53 vv 4-5
But God who is rich in mercy ... raised us up with him.
                                        Ephesians 2 vv 4-6

XL
I GREET YOU MARY.

A woman like us is in heaven, mother of God in Jesus Christ, forever contemplating him with her pure gaze.
She is our sister but also our mother, for every day she conceives us through her Son if we are open to his life.
Daughter of the earth, united in body and soul, her loving affection is continually offered to us all.
One cannot live without mum.

I greet you Mary.

Mary of Yes,
      refusing noes
      always accepting
love offered.

Silent Mary
      the silence of seeds
      growing in our land
      the Word of Life.

Beautiful Mary
      the beauty of light
      lighting up blank faces
      in the Sun of the Child.

Everyday Mary
      threading
      a thousand moments of the day
      into rosary beads.

Loving Mary
    giving us kisses
    flights of birds
    on dry foreheads

Smiling Mary
    living in flowers
    flowers to gather
    for passers-by

Weeping Mary
    giving rivers of tears
    to water
    dried up hearts.

Mary on high
    so highly placed
pray for me
    so badly placed
Mary remembering
    faithfully remembering
    remember me
    when with my heavy earthly feet
    I enter into *Life*.

I greet you Mary
    mother Mary
    beloved Mary
    so be it.

Mary said "my soul doth magnify the Lord".   *Luke vv 1 46-49*

When Jesus saw Mary and the disciple whom he loved standing by ...
                                      John 19 vv 26-27